I Don't Want to Die Alone!

TRUE
STORIES
OF ONLINE
DATING

Stacey Levin and Robin Mesger

Outskirts Press, Inc.
Denver, Colorado

I Don't Want to Die Alone!
True Stories of Online Dating

v4.0

Outskirts Press, Inc.
http://www.outskirtspress.com

ISBN: 978-1-4327-7339-7

PRINTED IN THE UNITED STATES OF AMERICA

What people are saying about **I Don't Want to Die Alone!:**

"Robin Mesger and Stacey Levin are the perfect literary tour guides into the world of online dating. Witty and slightly ribald, they turn even the most horrific internet hook-ups into fodder for their humorous take on looking for love by logging on."

Brad Bessey, Execuive Producer,
CBS's The Talk, Co-Executive Producer, Entertainment Tonight

"The days of traditional dating are over, so what's a single girl to do... hello, internet dating! Stacey and Robin capture the 21st century dating world with a collaboration of funny, entertaining, witty, charming, and sometimes heartbreaking, experiences."

Sarah Michelle Gellar, Actress

"Robin and Stacey have captured the humor and heartbreak of the hunt for Mr. or Ms. Right. The vignettes are sharp and well crafted, bringing the characters in I Don't Want to Die Alone! to life in a hugely entertaining way."

Cynthia Littleton, Variety

"Oh my God, this is high-larious! I think you have a definite hit on your hands. Funny, personal, touching, current and relevant - and I was surprised many times during each story – excellent!"

Kathy Najimy, Actress

This book is dedicated to our families, friends and everyone who is just a click away from finding true love online.

Stacey and Robin

Contents

Introduction 1
The Angry Little Man 5
eHarmony.com, Here I Come 11
You Have the Right to Remain Silent 17
Coitus Interruptus 23
Oy Vey 35
Match.com is Full of Shit - Allegedly 41
Dude Looks Like a Lady 49
From Russia With Love 55
Hide the Salami 61
Feets Don't Fail Me Now 65
Serial Dating 101 71
Match.com is Still (and Always Will Be) Full of Shit - Allegedly 75
I'm a Slave For You 81
Where is Waldo? 85
It Takes Two to Tango 91
Thar She Blows 97
Here Comes the Bride 103
The Return of Brian 107
Yabba, Dabba, Don't 117
Elvis' Date Has Left the Building 123
Happily Ever After? 129

A Country in Crisis 139
Let's Talk About Sex, Baby...147
Heaven Sent 151
Call the Authorities 165
Disclaimer...175

Introduction

So how many times have you heard this line: "how is it possible that you're still single?" We're two good looking, successful, smart, Jewish chicks from New York who moved to Los Angeles and totally have our shit together... more or less. I'm Robin, in my early forties with a killer rack, which is real, thank you very much. And I'm Stacey, mid thirties but look 22 even on a bad day and still get carded at the grocery store when I buy beer. To boot, we both have really cool jobs in the entertainment industry. You might think that's a plus, but in Los Angeles, it's a big minus. It limits the amount of eligible men we meet on a daily basis and makes us targets for the losers.

After four years, Robin finally dumped her lying, cheating boyfriend and after being pressured by almost everyone, decided to finally try online dating. Stacey, who dedicated her life to work, reluctantly agreed to try it as well. At first, we signed up for one site each, but things were moving slowly and we decided to expand our reach. Before we knew it, we were on everything – match.com, eHarmony, Jdate, yahoo, AOL personals, and singlesnet just to name a few.

Now you're thinking we got what we deserved because we posted all over the net. But wait, so did most of the guys we "met." For example, we both encountered nineinchesplus (and we're not making that up) on several sites along with papachulorockstar, hardonealways, deathcums4u and allday69. What started out as an alternative way to date in L.A. suddenly became a part of our daily routine.

It was like a drug addiction. At first we gave in because of all of the peer pressure – "Come on, just try it once. I swear you'll like it." Then we got a taste and it wasn't bad, so we started doing more and more – we went from one site to five sites in a matter of days. Then we couldn't stop thinking about it – Who emailed us today? Who viewed our profiles today? Did that guy we emailed respond? And if he didn't, then why not? IS MY PHOTO NOT GOOD ENOUGH? WHAT'S WRONG WITH ME?

Soon the addiction went to the next level. We started checking out our competition. Some sites won't let you do this, but thanks to match.com and Jdate, we got enough of a fix to compare ourselves to every other single woman in the state. What we discovered from our little investigation was that there were a lot of seemingly cool, pretty, smart, successful women in their 20's, 30's, 40's, and 50's who were in the exact same position as we were. However, there's one drawback to checking out other women – Robin still can't lose this bicurious girl from Florida who's actually smoking hot and been emailing her for the last six weeks. What this taught us is when you view someone's profile, they know you looked at them. This can be a disaster. (Yes, that's a warning!)

And, like an addiction, once we finally started to admit it to other people, we soon discovered that almost everybody we knew was also online looking for love. Over the last few years, in addition to our dating exploits, we have heard stories from women and men, straight and gay, which Lifetime could make into movies. This book is a tribute to those stories – some good, some bad and some unbelievable (but we swear they're all true.)

The Angry Little Man
Robin Goes on Her First match.com Date

For four years I dated a charming, fun, older man who turned out to be a major loser. He not only broke my heart, but he also destroyed my trust in men and confidence in myself. After finding out he was cheating on me with some Botoxed divorcee, I dumped his ass and spent the next six months feeling sorry for myself, crying and being depressed. My friends were getting fed up that I couldn't get past him and I wasn't going to meet anybody with red swollen eyes, so I decided the pity party was over. If Jennifer Aniston could recover after publically being cheated on and dumped by Brad Pitt, then I should be able to get it together, too. Because I lived in L.A. and worked crazy hours, it made it really difficult to meet a good man. So, I decided it was time to go online and match.com was my first choice.

I first met Bruce, a 45-year-old documentary producer, on match.com. His photo was cute, so I "winked" at him. Within one minute, he "winked" back. I scanned his profile (key word here is scanned, not read) and we soon exchanged some emails, then phone numbers. How exciting! My first match.com date was being planned. This was easier than I thought. What the hell was everyone complaining about? Clearly, I wouldn't be single for long.

Bruce called me and surprisingly enough, we had a really nice conversation... no awkward pauses, no stammering and no lack of topics to talk about. We made plans to meet for lunch at The Grove, an outdoor shopping mall with nice restaurants. I decided to actually read his profile in detail before heading out the door for my date. It said he was divorced, no kids, Jewish and wait a second... he's only 5'7? Ok, 5'7 wasn't that bad. I could live with that. I headed out to the Grove feeling confident, cute and um, well, tall.

So there I was standing in front of La Piazza wondering if everyone around me knew that I was waiting for my match.com date to meet me. Could they tell? Did it show on my face? It was like I was the only person there who didn't know who she's eating lunch with. What if that wasn't really Bruce in the photo? What if he was missing all of his front teeth? What if he had really bad body odor? Just as I was starting to spin out of control, I felt a tap on my shoulder, but when I turned around, nobody was there. What the hell? And then I looked down. Bruce. Standing tall at a whopping 5'3. Yep, 5'3. No where near 5'7. Ok, so let's take a minute to explain. I'm only 5'4 myself, however, I'm never without my heels, so on that day, I was about 5'8. I'm also on the thin side and Bruce's waist was smaller than mine. All in all, he could have fit under my armpit. But, on the bright side, he was good looking with dark hair - all on his head - a nice smile and a big nose, which just happens to be a personal preference of mine. He also had no detectable B.O. and he appeared to have all of his teeth. I told myself to keep an open mind, so I smiled my brightest smile and said "nice to meet you!" By the expression on his face, Bruce seemed happy with how I looked in person.

We ordered drinks and settled in to get to know each other. And boy, did I get to know Bruce. He never stopped talking. And you know the expression TMI - too much information? Bruce, if you ever read this – a word of advice: SHUT UP! I knew more about Bruce than his own mother did. Here's the condensed version: Bruce's first wife turned out to be a lesbian who left him for another women after 15 years of marriage. Bruce told me he was determined to get back at her. Umm... how, by dating men? This should have been my first red flag. After his first marriage failed, he decided he was going to find his high school sweetheart on classmates.com and he did. Turned out she was single, loaded, living in Brentwood and gorgeous. Bruce hit the jackpot. But alas, that relationship didn't work out and after only two years, not only did she leave Bruce, but it was for another woman (I swear I'm not making this up.) High School Sweetheart had lots of money, none of which she gave to Bruce in the divorce, so now 45-years-old and twice divorced, he was living in a guest house and looking for wife number three. Throughout the whole conversation, he kept reminding me that he did indeed really like women (apparently not as much as his ex-wives) and he was not bitter - really HE'S NOT BITTER he shouted as he stabbed the fork into the table repeatedly. Oh my God, I had to get the fuck out of there. By this point, I swore everyone else in the restaurant was staring at me. Did that lady at the next table hear him? Are they asking themselves why he's so small? Who is this raving, crazy manchild that blonde is sitting with?

Up to this point, I had barely said a word aside from the occasional "really," "uh huh" and "Bruce, it's time to order." I quickly ordered another glass of chardonnay (and keep 'em coming, lady) and a tuna nicoise salad. This is where Bruce, who probably weighed 100 pounds soaking wet, ordered the following: a bowl of minestrone soup, a Ceasar salad, chicken picatta and a side of pasta. WHAT? WHERE WAS HE GOING TO PUT ALL OF THIS? BUT MORE IMPORTANTLY, HOW LONG WAS IT GOING TO TAKE HIM TO EAT IT? Bruce asked me two questions about myself, then the conversation turned back to him, his life, his problems, his dreams and the fact that he really liked women. And I swear, he ate everything he ordered. EVERYTHING! Hmm, maybe he was bulimic. I waited and waited to see if he would excuse himself to go to the bathroom, but no such luck. As he scooped up the last of the pasta sauce with the last piece of Italian bread, I breathed a sigh of relief. Finally, lunch was coming to a close and I would soon be free. When the waitress approached, instead of asking her for the check, Bruce proceeded to order what I could only describe as the biggest fucking sundae I'd ever seen. Just watching him eat this monstrosity made me want to throw up. It must have had 16 scoops of ice cream, tons of whipped cream, a gallon of chocolate sauce and a jar of cherries. And...yes, he took one cherry, held it high above his mouth, "seductively" bit it off the stem and asked "did you like that tongue action?" Oh no, he didn't! Yeah, he did. I know you're asking why didn't I just leave? Because in my online dating naiveté, I didn't want to be rude. Big mistake! Big! Huge! My being polite cost me another 45 minutes of listening to Bruce's rant, raves and smacking of his lips with every spoonful of ice cream that went into his mouth. When the waitress returned with the check, I found myself noticing how pretty she was. Now I understood what happened with his ex-wives.

After all of this, you would think I earned a free lunch, right? Nope. Bruce asked me for half of the check. Considering his lunch cost $80 and mine was all of $15.95, I guess you could say Bruce got off pretty cheap. Wow, what a gentleman. As we were leaving the restaurant, I tried sprinting to my car. Maybe I could make a fast getaway with just a slight jog, but before I could run away, he said he had a wonderful time and wanted to see me again. At a loss for words along with that stupid naiveté, I said sure, give me a call. Hey, I had caller ID. No worries.

eHarmony.com, Here I Come
Stacey Takes the Plunge

For an entire year, Robin was after me to join online dating. Why? Because she'd been doing so well on it? No way, it was not for me. Dating was on the bottom of my list. I was so dedicated to my studio job, all I ever did was work. And if I wasn't at work, I was reading scripts all hours of the night. If I didn't have a successful career, then nothing else mattered. Plus I had a dog, good friends and a healthy social life. The last thing I needed was a man... or I should say a full-time man. I did have a friend, Matt, who lived out of state. While he lived temporarily in L.A., we dated and after he went home, we would hang out when he visited. See? Life was just fine.

Well, famous last words. After a long day at work, I came home to find my beautiful puppy had taken a flying leap off the couch and broken both of his back legs... again. For all of the money I had spent on this dog, I could have adopted one of Brad and Angelina's African kids and at least had someone to take care of me in my old age. OK, at least I still had my friends. That is, the ones who weren't married, having kids or dating like crazy off the internet. To sum it up: I was facing a huge vet bill, friendless and trying to make a long distance relationship work. Life SUCKED and here came Robin with her mantra: You Need to Go Online! Ah, what the fuck. I had nothing else to do. At the time, "Jersey Shore: Season Two" was still a few months away, so eHarmony, here I come. The people in those damn commercials looked so happy and there was something about Dr. Warren I trusted. I just had to fill out the application and they would do all of the work. How hard could it be?

Have you ever filled out an eHarmony application? I was convinced Dr. Warren must have started his career working at the IRS or some place known for creating an incredible amount of useless, pointless, inane paperwork. I'd never answered so many questions about myself before – my SATs took less time to complete than my eHarmony form. Ok, here's how it went: Section 1 was 65 questions on self-description where you use a rating system of a scale of 1-7, one being "not at all," four being "somewhat" and 7 being "very." Did I consider myself stylish? I don't know. Um, how about 4? Do I think I'm beautiful? Sure, don't we all? 7. Am I shapely? What the hell does that mean? Um, 4 again. Holy crap. Am I fit? Am I restless? Am I wise? Do I like order and respect? Can I take a conversation to a higher level? Am I frugal? Quarrelsome? Submissive? AHHHHHHH! Whew, finished. That wasn't so bad. Wait, I was only 37% finished. Jesus Christ.

Ok, Section 2 was 65 questions about personal characteristics with a scale of 1-7, one being "rarely," 4 being "occasionally" and 7 being "almost always." Here's a sample of what I had to answer about my feelings over the last month: I was satisfied with my level of emotional development; I viewed myself as well adjusted (well, I did until I started taking this quiz); I like to think outside the box; I liked to take time to smell the roses; I'm misunderstood; I'm plotted against. Wait, was I plotted against? Like I need that to happen, too. Oh God, I don't know... Time to catch my breath because I had to be finished now, right? Nope. Only 55% done. Wait, I think I just saw a promo for "Jersey Shore: Season Two" – how long have I been doing this?

Let's jump to Section 8 (Yes, you read correctly. I said "8."), which was about my personality. Oh, good it's true or false – there are only two answers. As I read through the list of statements, some of them bear repeating. Ready? I always read ALL of the warning literature on side effects before taking medicine. (Please tell me how this is going to help me find a boyfriend.) I like people because they're popular with others. (No, I like to hang out with losers.) If a store clerk gave me too much change, I might keep it without telling her. (Hello? Need to pay for my dog's surgery. Of course I'm keeping it.)

Section 10 – I'm 88% there! Woo-hoo. It must have been days at this point that I had been sitting in front of the computer. I hadn't even fed the dog. This was all about my living skills. Out of 75 choices, I could only pick three and yes, these three were among the selection: remaining calm yet resilient during a crisis (ok, that's a good one), finding pleasure and contentment in simple things (sure, sounds reasonable), and car maintenance and repair. Um, what? I'd like to see the results of Dr. Warren's personality profile. For him to have devised this test convinced me he must NOT be reading the side effects of some of his medication.

Finally, the last question. The very last question. I've got to keep going. I've come too far to stop now. Must – finish - profile... how much had I completed? I wearily look up at my percentage – 99.8% completed. Oh for the love of God. How far do I want my date to live? 5-10 miles? 10-20 miles? Within 400 miles? In this country? On this planet? In our universe? Can I just check all? No, not an option – I'll say within 50 miles. Hell if I'm really going to drive 50 miles, but after 82 hours of filling out this stupid test, I figured I should at least keep the options open.

I then posted my photo, hit "send" and waited for Dr. Warren to send me a fantastic selection of eligible men within 50 miles of my apartment, who read all of the side effects literature, stopped to smell the roses and kept their cars in pristine condition.

As I put myself to bed exhausted from self-examination, I dreamt of all of the men Dr. Warren would send me in the morning. Like the night before Christmas, visions of profiles danced in my head. And when I checked my email the next day, eHarmony did not disappoint. The email read: eHarmony match found! Wait, only one? Really? In all of California, there's only one guy who matched my profile? Well, ok, it only took one, right? This could be THE one. I hit the link and as I waited for my match to materialize, I felt optimistic about Dr. Warren's incredible skills. Filling out that profile and paying the way above average monthly fee was going to be worth it. Wait, here he comes... his name was Bill, he's 37 and really cute and lives in... wait for it... Idaho? Boise fucking Idaho? I said 50 miles, not 500 miles!

Well, after waiting three months, I had not been matched with anyone since Bill. Apparently, I was unmatchable. However, while I was waiting for eHarmony to make my dreams come true, I discovered there are a gazillion other dating sites and so I was about to take the plunge again.

You Have the Right to Remain Silent Scott's Got the NYPD... Blues

So reader, we are leaving L.A. and taking you 3,000 miles across the country to New York City. The city that never sleeps. The city where a gazillion people walk the streets each day. The city where our friend Scott decided to join Yahoo Personals to find his very own Statue of Liberty. A woman who was strong, reliable and dependable, but who also happened to live on Long Island. Scott was 32, divorced, no kids, and good looking with a great job. So what was the problem? Even though he worked in the city, he really wanted to date someone who lived near him. He was tired of dating women in the five boroughs. Long Island was made up of two huge counties and Yahoo Personals could help him navigate them. So, after a number of bad blind dates and too many nights being cruised by the cougars at the TGI Fridays and Applebees, Scott decided to give the internet a try.

As soon as Scott posted his profile, the floodgates opened. Women from all over New York State came calling–Manhattan, Staten Island, Westchester, Albany, Syracuse and even Utica. Needless to say, Scott had a lot of choices. While he wasn't willing to date someone 350 miles away in a city that bordered on Canada, he was willing to go anywhere between Nassau and Suffolk county. And there she was – KeytoMyHeart516. She was an adorable redhead with an infectious smile, and her profile couldn't have been more perfect. She was a homebody who loved spending cozy nights in front of the fire, home cooked meals and watching old movies – all things Scott loved to do. She had a lucrative sales job, wasn't into the bar scene and refused to date anyone who "liked long walks on the beach" – finally, a girl who saw through a cheesy online profile.

After a few emails, they decided to exchange phone numbers. Their conversations flowed easily and Scott had a great feeling about KeytoMyHeart516 a.k.a. Julie. They made plans to meet that weekend at a restaurant in Long Beach. They spoke the whole week leading up to the date and for the first time in a long time, Scott was excited about meeting someone. Friday before the big date, he got a call from Julie while he was riding home from work on the Long Island Railroad. She had to cancel their date because her neighbor had a family emergency and she was needed to watch their dog. Julie said she felt very badly about canceling and since she was stuck in the house for the night, she invited Scott over. Not wanting this date to be just a hook up, Scott politely declined and they rescheduled for the following Tuesday.

When Tuesday arrived, Scott called Julie to suggest they meet at Prego's, a popular restaurant located close to both their neighborhoods. Julie loved the place, but thought it would be much more intimate if he came over to her place for a bottle of wine first. In fact, she insisted he go to her place for drinks.

Insisted? Her place? At this point, Scott's penis started to do the talking. He liked this girl, but if all she was interested in doing was hooking up, who was he to argue? Now readers, this is where men and women really differ. A woman would never, ever go to a guy's house for a first date when they met on the internet unless she wanted to be the front page story of The New York Post or be the topic of an episode of *Law & Order: SVU*. That's why women don't have penises.

But Scott did have a penis and by now, he was thinking with it as he drove to Julie's house. He was impressed when he pulled up to her massive condo complex – this place had multiple buildings and garages. It would probably be easier to get in and out of Fort Knox than this development. Not knowing exactly where he was going, Scott called Julie to ask her to meet him at the guest parking entrance. She said she was still getting dressed, so she would talk him through the directions. A few seconds later, Scott thought he might have to get the navigation system out of his car. After walking what seemed like a mile and half, he finally reached Julie's apartment... and he was excited. He was ready to meet the sweet, funny red head with whom he'd spent many nights talking to on the phone. All was right in the world.

Ding dong.

When Julie opened the door, Scott couldn't believe what he was seeing. She was stunning. She had the bluest eyes he'd ever seen, a perfect nose and boy, the smile... her photos were the real deal. They hugged and he stepped back to check her out. A petite, tight body clad in a cute, black halter dress with strappy sandals and an ankle bracelet. She was so... wait,

Scott's thoughts were interrupted as he did a double take. And then a triple take. What the hell kind of ankle bracelet was that? It was big and clunky with a blinking red light in the corner. Shit! Oh, this chick had a bracelet around her ankle all right. But it was a FUCKING HOUSE ARREST BRACELET. WTF? Lindsay Lohan's bracelet wasn't this big.

While Scott freaked, Julie tried to explain that she had a little, um, "mishap" with the law and instead of doing jail time, she chose house arrest. Did she rob a bank? Knock off a 7-11? Murder someone? Perhaps someone she met on the internet? Maybe she was she an internet serial killer who dismembered bodies in her bathtub. Fuck! Not wanting to find out, he dropped the flowers at her feet and took off down the hall.

He made a mad dash down the hallway, which quickly became the hallway straight out of The Shining – it just got longer and longer the more he ran. Julie started to chase after him, but just as he reached the elevator, he heard this piercing beeping fill his ears. Oh dear God, she just set off her bracelet. "Please, Scott," she begged, "I can only go 25 feet down the hall before the cops get here." Oh Christ. No one would ever believe this happened to him. He didn't want to believe this was happening to him. As he ran through the maze of buildings and driveways to get to his car, he wondered if that was her real apartment or if the cops had stashed her there because even Al Capone himself wouldn't be able to find his way in or out of this complex.

Dripping in sweat, Scott finally reached his car and caught his breath. It all came crashing down on him – flashes of conversation raced through his mind: she didn't like the bar scene (cause she couldn't get to it), she liked watching old movies (cause she couldn't get out to see a new one), she was in sales (that she made from her home phone) and she was a homebody (no shit, Sherlock.) For fuck's sake, her name was KeytoMyHeart – how obvious was that? And she didn't like long walks on the beach? Well, that made sense because the beach was definitely more than 25 feet from her apartment. Then Scott started laughing. He went online to find his Statue of Liberty and he ended up meeting someone who was anything but free. Oh well, back to the boroughs and the blind dates – at least those girls weren't wanted felons.

Coitus Interruptus
Courtney Meets Malibu Tex

When our friend Courtney told us she signed up for americansingles.com, we were floored. If a woman like Courtney needed online dating help, the whole female race was in trouble. Let's take a second to describe Courtney. How should we put it? Well, she's STUNNING. And we're not exaggerating at all. If Brad Pitt and Charlize Theron had a daughter, she would look like Courtney (no offense, Shiloh.) Courtney was in her mid-30's, about 5'7, maybe 115 pounds, naturally blonde and blue eyed and all around perfect. She's also a successful actress to boot – and one of the most down to earth people you'd ever meet. So why would a woman like Courtney need online dating? Hey, dating in L.A. for the average woman is hard enough, but dating in L.A. as a beautiful actress who didn't want to grace the pages of tmz.com everyday, it's even harder. She purposely didn't post her photo on the site because she wanted to finally meet a guy who wasn't asking her out because of how she looked. And she thought she met the perfect guy when she met Brandon.

Brandon was in his late-30's, tall, handsome and built like a football player. He was a self described "oil and gas man" straight from Texas – and no, he didn't pump it. Courtney found herself a bona fide J.R. Ewing! And the rest of us wanted to kill ourselves. He was rich – filthy, disgustingly rich. Brandon told her about his four houses he owned in the L.A. area and his wealthy father, a multi-billion dollar oil mogul who still lived in Texas. On their first date, he gave her his father's website so she could check the business out for herself because that was also the company where Brandon worked. She checked and yep, it was a multi-billion dollar oil and gas company. Courtney was the farthest thing from a gold digger. She found Brandon really attractive, filled with Southern charm and by the end of the date, Courtney didn't care if he worked at the local Mobil station, she was hooked.

For their next date, Brandon suggested they meet for dinner then see a play at an upscale theater in Brentwood. Courtney was thrilled and eagerly awaited the night. However, on the morning of their date, Brandon called and told her he couldn't make dinner, but could they meet at the theater instead at exactly 8pm because he had a meeting. Since the curtain rose at 8, Courtney knew there was a big chance they wouldn't get seated if they arrived at the last minute, so she innocently asked if he could duck out of his meeting early – after all, he did work for his father.

Brandon: *"Oh, I don't work for my father. I would never work for that man – we have a very contentious relationship."*

Say what? He spent half of the first date telling her about his rich dad and their uber-oil company. Now he said he didn't work for him? Ok, so what exactly did Brandon do? Brandon claimed he owned his *own* oil and gas company. Huh?

Brandon promised they'd get in to see the show, so she waited in the lobby for him to arrive. 8pm. 8:05pm. 8:10pm. Tick tock! The ushers had been graciously holding the curtain because they recognized Courtney, but she was mortified. Just as she was about to leave, Brandon came rushing to the entrance. He apologized for being late and turning on his Southern charm, and a brand new drawl that Courtney hadn't heard before, Brandon asked the usher to seat Courtney in any available seat while he bought the tickets. Ok, say what again? He had to first buy the tickets? Who went to the theater, especially this theater, had someone wait for the curtain to rise and didn't even have the fucking tickets? Courtney was so embarrassed, she just thanked the usher for his patience and said they would leave. So instead of seeing the latest play, Courtney and Brandon ended up in Starbucks. Starbucks? Was that the best he could do after that giant screw-up? Things that made us go hmmm.

Even after the play disaster, Courtney still liked Brandon and wanted to give him another chance. After all, everyone made mistakes. Brandon knew he had to make it up to her, so he suggested they see the Dali exhibit at the Los Angeles County Museum of Art since he was Courtney's favorite artist. Courtney was impressed that Brandon brought up this event, which had a month-long waiting list. Once again, he suggested they meet in the lobby and once again, Brandon was late. 20 minutes late. Was this a pattern with this guy? Meanwhile,

Courtney was standing in line so she could get tickets. She was almost at the ticket window when Brandon came rushing through the door. He apologized and told her she didn't need to wait in line. He spoke quickly to a museum employee and they were ushered into the exhibit.

Courtney: *I can't believe you were able to buy tickets in advance.*
Brandon: *Nah, babe, I told them we were members of the press. Works every time.*

Unable to speak or move, Courtney was horrified as Brandon continued into the museum. Did he really scam their way into this event instead of paying for two $15 tickets? But he was a multi-millionaire. Wasn't he?

At this point, we were sure Brandon was toast. Courtney had to be done with him after this latest stunt. So imagine our surprise when she told us she was going out with him again. Ok, ladies, we had all been there. He said he was sorry and Courtney was lonely. Maybe the third time would be the charm. Well, as long as there were no tickets involved. Fine, go out with him again. Who were we to judge?

The next date was dinner. Brandon said he'd pick her up at 6:30pm and Courtney suggested Vermont, an upscale restaurant in her neighborhood. And since Brandon had yet to spend any of his millions on her, she thought she earned it. While she waited for him, she tried to get reservations but to no avail, and she settled for another restaurant nearby. Miracles of miracles, Brandon arrived ON TIME and PICKED HER UP. Seriously, a miracle! He was already steps ahead of the last two dates.

Courtney: *I couldn't get a reservation at Vermont because they were booked, so I got us a table at a French place down the street.*

Brandon: *No reservation? That's impossible. There's always a table for people like us.*

Courtney: *Um, what does that mean?*

Brandon: *It means there's always room for couples that look like us.*

Courtney was flabbergasted by his remarks. Who said things like that? Brandon assured her they could get into Vermont without a problem. Stunned by his arrogance, Courtney agreed to let him try. Maybe he would buy his way into a table because he hadn't bought anything else so far. As they approached the restaurant, Brandon noted the menu in the window and all of the color drained from his face. Hey, we said Vermont was upscale. And suddenly there was a mighty change of heart.

Brandon: *Eh, this place isn't my style. The French place looks good enough – let's just go there.*

Courtney was so relieved that Brandon wasn't going to embarrass them, she chose not to call him out on his earlier remarks. Immediately after being seated, Brandon frantically asked the waiter for some sugar. They hadn't even had time to get the bread basket and water put on the table. What did he need sugar for? Maybe he was hypo-glycemic?

Brandon: *Dude, sugar. Need some right now. Got any sugar? Sugar?*

Waiter: *Sir, what kind of sugar? A packet? A cube? Raw?*

Brandon: *I just need SUGAR! Can you get me some SUGAR NOW!!!*

Thinking Brandon was about to go into a diabetic coma, Courtney told the waiter to bring whatever they had available. He brought Brandon three kinds of sugar and she watched carefully as he slowly pulled a packet of sugar to his lips. And no, he did not suck down the crystals in a desperate effort to keep his body from going into shock. Instead, he actually spit his gum into the wrapper and placed it on the table for all to see.

Courtney: *What are you doing??*
Brandon: *Oh, I need to throw out my gum and didn't want to spit it out on the floor. I always use sugar packets.*

WTF? Really? Was this normal on any level? Ok, well, really wealthy people were known to be eccentric, so maybe this was just one of Brandon's quirks. Right? It's just a quirk? Please? Then it was time to order. All 115 pounds of Courtney was starving by this point so she ordered a full meal starting with appetizers. And then it was Brandon's turn. He proceeded to order a cup of onion soup. And? And nothing. That was all he wanted. One small, tiny cup of onion soup. Not even a bowl. Were you trying to tell us that one cup of beef broth with some onion slices and cheese was all this guy was going to eat? A guy who was built like Refrigerator Perry and knew all along they were going out to dinner? That was ridiculous.

Courtney: *What do you mean that's all you're going to have?*
Brandon: *Yeah, I don't like to eat this late.*
Courtney: *Um, it's 7pm.*
Brandon: *Yes, but it's 9pm in Texas.*

Having no response, she asked the waiter to bring her a double vodka martini – very dry. Since this was their fourth date, Courtney asked Brandon to finally tell her how old he was. For some reason, he would never just say it.

Brandon: *I told you I'm in my 30's*
Courtney: *Why is this so hard for you? I'm an actress and I told you my real age. Tell me yours. Here, I'll start the sentence for you. I am 30....?*
Brandon: *Fine, I'm 39.*
Courtney: *And I was born in 19....?*
Brandon: *Ok, 1979.*

Wait. Stop the presses. Being 38 in 2010 means you're born in 1972, not 1979. Was this guy really just 31 years old? But why would he lie?

Courtney: *That makes you 31 years old.*
Brandon: *No, it doesn't.*
Courtney: *Yeah, it does. Hello? Do the math.*
Brandon: *What does it matter? Age is just a number. Ah, I was just kidding with you anyway. I know how much you wanted to know. I'm really 39, I swear.*

At this point, Courtney's radar kicked in and she knew Brandon was lying, but why? And what else was he lying about? Who was this guy? And why was she still so attracted to him? And after Brandon paid the bill and he asked her out again, why, oh why, did she say yes? (Dear reader, believe us, we were asking her the same question.)

Well, the only way to explain it is like this – and ladies, we're sure most of you can relate. She was still bored and lonely; he was good looking and there was something still mysterious about him that kind of turned her on. Plus, she felt as if she put enough time into this, she should get something out of it. Because after all, they were already past the third date and we all knew what meant. She wanted to see him naked.

For their next date, Brandon suggested he make her dinner in his Malibu beach house (one of the many houses he claimed to have owned.) Nothing spoke romance more than dinner in Malibu in a beautiful house overlooking the Pacific Ocean. Courtney was excited, but as she drove up the path leading to the house, she noticed how quiet and dark the street was. If she listened very carefully, she could hear the ocean and the coyote howling on the next hill.

Brandon greeted her at the door of a house that could have easily been used on the set of Melrose Place. It was beautifully decorated and filled with expensive furniture and artwork. The only problem was that it didn't look like anyone actually lived there. Sure, a few of Brandon's things were carefully strewn in places, but it looked more like a model home than anything else.

Dinner was nicely set up in a very spacious dining room and it seemed like Brandon really went all out to impress her. After they ate, he suggested he show her the upstairs because the view was spectacular. (Cue porn music – bow, chika, bow, bow). Obviously, Courtney was about to get some and she knew it, so she agreed. As he led her up the spiral staircase, she couldn't help but notice there were no pictures of anyone on the walls. In fact, there were no pictures any where aside from one or two small framed photos on the dresser. Why was Courtney feeling as if those photos came with the frames? Before she could say anything, Brandon kissed her and suddenly it didn't matter.

Now, because Courtney was a good friend of ours who we'd like to keep, we're going to be very delicate in describing what happened next. Let's just say things were moving along nicely for Courtney and Brandon and at the most inopportune time of their loud tryst, someone burst through the front door of the house and shouted "What's going on in here?" WTF? Courtney instantly panicked as her heart started to pound. Brandon jumped up and ran out of the room without one stitch of clothing. Courtney immediately started to get dressed as different scenarios ran through her head. Were they being robbed? Were they being videotaped? Were they there to chop her and Brandon into tiny pieces to be thrown into the Malibu Bay? Where the fuck was her phone so she could call the police??

Brandon: *Whoa, dude, that was weird. That was my neighbor.*
Courtney: *Your fucking neighbor? What kind of neighbor enters your house in the middle of the night?*
Brandon: *Yeah, I know, right? Strange, huh? No biggie. Happens all the time. So, come on, let's finish what we started.*
Courtney: *Are you kidding me?*

At that moment, a flash went through Courtney's mind and suddenly she didn't think this was Brandon's house. And, when she got in her car to drive away, she had a feeling he'd be right behind her. Now truly afraid, she decided to leave with as little issue as possible.

Courtney: *You know, it's late already and I have an early audition tomorrow. And it'll take me an hour to get home, so I should be going.*

Oddly, Brandon didn't argue and helped her gather her things. He walked her to the car and as they were saying goodbye, Brandon commented on how eerily quiet it was outside. Hello, this was your neighborhood! Wouldn't you know if it's quiet outside?? Mortified and scared, Courtney didn't respond and got the hell out of dodge. The last thing she could deal with that night was the thought that his neighbors probably heard them having sex. And there was no mistaking it for the coyote howling on the next hill.

The next day Courtney told us the whole sordid story and realized there was something really off about this guy. You think? She wanted no part of him anymore – looks and charm could only get him so far. So while she composed her "Dear John" email to get rid of him, we got the address from her and drove to the house. There was no way we were going to let this opportunity pass us by. We'd love to tell you we found Brandon watering his flowers or mowing his lawn or even washing his car in the driveway. But instead what we found was a big fat "For Sale" real estate sign out front. Apparently, there was an open house the day before. Things that made us go hmmm all over again.

A week later, Courtney was having lunch with a friend who lived in Malibu and she brought up her experience with

Brandon. Her friend immediately knew who he was and called him Malibu Brandon. Apparently, everyone in Malibu was hip to Malibu Brandon – a total loser without a dime to his name who scammed pretty women he thought he could use for money and a potential career. Even as Courtney began to describe him, her friend stopped her and finished the description. Everyone really did know the Texan Malibu Brandon. And thankfully, Courtney saved herself from becoming Malibu Barbie. Whew!

Oy Vey
Robin Joins Jdate.com

Even though I'm a Jewish woman from Brooklyn, New York, Jewish men just never appealed to me. I always went for the Italian boys or the wannabe rock stars. So in my 40's and not knowing how much longer my poor mother could beg me to meet a nice Jewish guy, I bit the bullet and joined Jdate.com. Imagine my surprise when I found a plethora of guys who were just my type – dark hair, dark skin and big noses. I wasn't ready to break out the Matzah and the Manichevitz yet, but this site looked promising. Within the first week, I was already flirting and emailing with some really good looking, successful men located within 50 miles of my West Hollywood neighborhood.

Jdate #1 was named Scott, a tall 44-year-old lawyer. His profile was cleverly written. He had never been married and didn't have any children. After spending an hour on the phone, we decided to meet for a drink. He suggested the Urth Café, a trendy, organic coffee and herbal tea house. No, no, no, no! Drinks by my definition contained alcohol and there was nothing organic about my taste, but I went anyway.

Standing in front of the restaurant watching pseudo hippies and tree-huggers discuss the environment while drinking over-priced herbal beverages, I was anticipating an interesting date with Scott. That's when I noticed a really good looking gay man bouncing down the street. He was tall, slim, with dark hair, a big nose and holy shit! It was Scott. He skipped his way up to the front door, introduced himself and we ordered drinks. He got a Divine Spice Herbal Chai Latte. What the hell was that? Wait, wasn't that what Will ordered every episode of "Will and Grace?" I took my Poland Springs bottle of water and joined him at the table.

The conversation was ok, nothing too noteworthy until Scott asked to see my jewelry. Why? He said he loved women's jewelry and was fascinated by the way women wore different items. Oooookkkayyyy. He then asked if I wanted to go window shopping. Ok, sure, why not? As we proceeded to leave the Café, he became enamored by my purse and told me that aside from women's jewelry, he loved how many different types of purses women had to choose from and how important an accessory it was in a woman's life. Dude, let's go window shop you a man-bag. At this point, it was safe to say my mother wouldn't have to call a Rabbi any time soon.

Knowing this wasn't going to go any anywhere, I tried to pleasantly keep the conversation flowing as we stopped at every friggin' store on the block. Scott had running commentary on everything – women's clothing, furniture, artwork, perfumes. Weren't there any sporting goods stores on this street? Nah, because he wasn't interested in sports. In fact, he only watched travel and decorating shows on TV. So I'm guessing his favorite team wasn't the Giants or the Mets, it was probably Dolce & Gabanna. He told me he'd been on Jdate for a year and while he was looking for the woman of his dreams, right now he was seeking a travel companion because he loved to travel. He and his friend just got back from a trip to a bed and breakfast in the mountains where Scott discovered that two men in their 40's traveling alone raised a lot of eyebrows. Well, dude, not if you go to Fire Island, Miami or San Francisco! It was time to end this date as I was clearly with a Jewish boy who was definitely into other Jewish boys and way deep in his colorful and well accessorized closet.

Jdate #2 was Ira. With that name, you're already on guard, right? From Ira's small picture and profile, he was really cute and had potential. We exchanged a few emails and were ready to meet at a restaurant known for good wine and food. I arrived first and ordered a glass of wine while I waited at the bar. Ten minutes later, in walks Ira who did resemble his photo which was a relief. The bartender asked Ira what he'd like to drink and Ira made this poor guy recite the 150 red wines they carried. And when this guy finally finished, Ira asked for the wine list anyway before finally deciding on one. When the bartender asked if we would be eating, Ira quickly answered no. Um... hello, I was sitting there, too.

I decided to start the conversation with a seemingly innocent question – what brought you to L.A.? In the most nasally, whiny voice I'd ever heard, Ira proceeded to give me the in-depth, play by play breakdown of how he got to L.A. from Washington D.C. mile by mile. Here's the short of it: Ira was living in D.C. when his girlfriend broke up with him so he answered an ad on craigslist for someone who needed a partner to drive cross county. Ira packed up his cats (CATS?? Deal-breaker right there) and hit the road. In the five years he had lived in Los Angeles, he's lived in every possible neighborhood in the area. Seriously. West L.A., North Hollywood, Eagle Rock, Los Feliz, Encino, Hollywood... the list just went on. The only place he hadn't set up camp was in Compton. And just today, his roommate (ROOMMATE? You're 45-years-old!) and his wife (WAIT, THE ROOMMATE HAS A WIFE? WASN'T THAT TWO ROOMMATES?) were divorcing and Ira would have to once again pack up his cats and find a new place to live. I couldn't bring myself to ask how many cats he actually had.

With the most sad sack demeanor I'd ever seen, he next started to discuss his lofty career goals. Just for the record, he had yet to ask anything about me. According to his profile, he was in sales and technically, he was. He told me he sold ad space for the Pennysaver, a free community newspaper. But he knew that job wasn't allowing him to really use his talents so he was very excited because he had a good interview coming up with a company that sold janitorial and plumbing supplies to restaurants and hotels. Dream big, Ira, reach for the stars. It was definitely time for another drink.

The bartender set down my second glass of wine and when he placed the check, Ira told him I would be taking care of it. The bartender looked at me and mouthed "I'm sorry." You cheap, toilet brush selling little Willy Loman loser! While Ira was describing in-depth the merits of In-and-Out burger vs. McDonald's, I pulled $20 out of my wallet, downed the full glass of wine in one gulp and walked out mid-sentence.

After Jdates #3, #4, #5 and #6, I can honestly say I had tried. Someone please bring my mother her medication because I am done with Jdate and the Jews. No Mrs. Robin Goldfarb any time soon.

Match.com is Full of Shit - Allegedly Stacey Gets Hi"jac"ked

So remember how I said I would take the plunge again? Well, I found my way to match.com in a less than traditional way. My friend Nick, an amazingly sweet guy who deserved a great girlfriend, thought he found one on match.com. Nick dropped by my office and couldn't wait to show me Miss Right, so he told me to sign on to the site. Unfortunately for Nick, when I tried to look at the site, it made me put in my information and requirements of what I was looking for. Thinking it was no big deal, I did. When it still wouldn't let me look, exasperated Nick grabbed the keyboard and just signed on with his log-in information.

As we waited for Nick's match page to appear, he was practically giddy talking about Miss Right – she's so pretty, she's so smart, they'd gone out three times already and hang on, her photo should be coming up any minute now. OH NO! Because I tried signing on with my information, Nick was now being matched with all of the perfect men in L.A. who were between the ages of 32-40, non-smoking, single or divorced. "What the fuck!" screamed Nick. "Now people are gonna think I'm into dudes! Get it off my profile!" Wait a minute, Nick, some of these guys were pretty cute. So after he showed me his woman, we signed off before anyone else in L.A. thought Nick was gay.

However, match.com refused to believe poor Nick and started sending him all of his "male" matches in the area, which Nick then forwarded to me for my consideration. Ok, but let's take a minute to think about this. Match.com charges about $40 a month and they couldn't take one second to re-read Nick's profile and realize he's clearly not a woman searching for a man within 25 miles of zip code 90068? Match.com red flag #1.

On the other hand, these guys were nice looking, seemed normal and wait a minute, I thought I knew one of them. I clicked on his photo and sure enough, it was a business associate named JT whom I met months earlier in a meeting. JT was a smart, educated, good looking, successful lawyer – maybe this site had a better selection of men than the other ones. This had to be a sign, right? I had plenty of friends that would be perfect for JT. If I couldn't find myself a date online, then I'd hook up my friends. That had to be good for my karma. Hey God, did you catch that? (Hello? Dog still needs surgery.)

Because I wasn't officially a match.com member, the site wouldn't allow me to email JT. I thought about asking Nick to email him for me, but the mix-up had already been way too traumatic for very heterosexual Nick. Since I had the perfect woman for JT and Lord knows I needed the brownie points, I decided to join the cult that is match.com – oops, I meant the site. After all, if a guy like JT was on here looking for love, it couldn't be that bad. And unlike eHarmony, I got to pick out the man of my dreams. Suck it, Dr. Warren and Boise-fucking-Idaho.

While I perused the hundreds of eligible men on this site, I got my first five "winks." For those of you who are happily married and secure with your man, a "wink" is an easy way to let another member know someone is interested. And sadly, Nick has since received ten "winks" from really hot guys. (Oh, the humanity.) But back to me - I received five "winks"! This was so easy... and then I looked at them. "Wink" #1 was a bald, overweight 55-year-old man. (Eww.) "Wink" #2 was from Amarillo, TX. (Could he be any farther away? I might as well go to Boise.) "Wink" #3 had been married twice and only separated from his third wife. (I know what you're thinking – it wasn't Bruce.) "Wink" #4 was an attractive man from Russia who didn't speak English and only needed $1000 to come to America. (No commentary necessary.) "Wink" #5 was a hot, 35-year-old entrepreneur from Sherman Oaks with a great smile. His screen name was yankeefan. Now we're talking.

I immediately "winked" back and checked out his profile. Wow! He had a bachelor's and master's degree. He'd traveled the world to places I needed to look up in an atlas and he was the most physically fit human being on the planet – he ran, he surfed and he skied - all in the same day. He's climbed every mountain, sailed every sea and was in training for the next triathlon. The last book he read was Snow by Orhan Pamuk. (What the hell was that?) Would it matter that the last book I read was Twilight?

While waiting for Mr. Perfect to "wink" back, I decided to do some exploring. This "winking" thing was really easy. I started "winking" at every good looking guy I came across. My finger was out of control – I "winked" up, I "winked" down, I "winked" to the left, I "winked" to the right. I'd become a "wink" freak! If this were a Ms. Pac Man game, my score would be record-breaking! Finally, I managed to tear myself away from the computer to wait to see if any of this "winking" actually worked.

One week later… a few winks back, but nothing to write home about. Still, there were a few, so maybe I should read their profiles since I was "winking" based on their photos. (Ok, fine, women can be superficial, too.) After checking out several of these guys, I noticed a pattern – they were all lawyers, doctors, entrepreneurs (translation – unemployed), artists or successfully self-employed. They have all traveled the world extensively from the Great Wall of China to the hilltops of Matchupichu to the Australian Barrier Reef. Didn't anybody just go to Hawaii any more? They were all well educated, had great senses of humor and were extremely well read – usually with books I'd never heard of before. And every one of them featured a photo of himself snowboarding in action. Match.com red flag #2 – none of these guys sounded real.

Three weeks later… after all of this "winking" crap, I still hadn't had a date off match.com. There had been some emails, but these guys just didn't follow through. I think I would rather spend my $40 a month renewing my Netflix subscription. I stopped almost all of my match.com activity. It was time to pull the plug on match.com. Then I got an email from Jacques880 – not a "wink," a full-on articulate and intriguing email. Jac, as he signed his email, should be on the cover of GQ or posing for the next Calvin Klein underwear ad. I didn't even bother to read his profile – he was the most gorgeous man I'd ever laid eyes on. I immediately emailed back. We were going to have beautiful children.

One week later... still hadn't heard back from Jac. But he emailed me first and I just paid for another month of match.com, dammit. Should I email him again? I already named our kids – Amelie and Pierre (French like their dad.) Maybe he found someone else. Maybe he's not even on match.com anymore. A guy who looked like this wasn't going to be single for long... time to really read his profile. As his page opened, I couldn't believe what I saw. In the essay portion of his profile, he goes on for ten paragraphs. Ten! Here are some of the highlights: he quotes both Robert Louis Stevenson and Jean-Paul Sartre (there's the French connection) and describes himself as "gentle, warm, attractive, gracious, idealistic, sentimental, creative, sensual, self-aware, generous, reliable, easy-going, thoughtful, passionate, refined, spiritual (but not religious), curious about almost everything, extremely affectionate, highly expressive and single." Well, wasn't being single a pre-requisite?

He's well-traveled (of course): "It's hard to be bored in this world! I do a lot of traveling, have been to S.America, Europe, Asia, Australasia (sic), Hawaii often." Where the hell was Australasia? And he wouldn't be on match.com if he wasn't well-educated in both the UK and Ivy League schools - "I have taken many courses since, including anthropology, neurophysiology, poetry writing, atomic physics. Learning new things is a real kick." Atomic physics? Oh, come on.

Apparently, he "seeks epiphanies and revelations at every turn" which included "exploring the nooks and crannies of the city; enchanting bookstores; fiery sunsets and foggy moons; cozy fireplaces; charming restaurants; country strolls; the roar of the ocean and the rhapsody of the city; flea markets brimming with antiques and other things quaint or old-fashioned; yoga; hot cocoa and chocolate ice cream sodas; Christmastime; belletristic prose (a fancy way of saying "essays"); puppies and kittens; entertaining friends; savoring movies, plays, concerts, museums, photography, or anything else artistic; volunteering with underprivileged kids; frolicking and picnicking in the state Park; curling up with a good book in one hand and a good snuggler in the other; and occasionally treating her to a long, luscious, languorous massage - though not necessarily in that order."

Really, Jac, really?

And here was the clincher. He ended this piece of belletristic prose (thank God he explained that above) with: "My wife" are two of the most beautiful words in the English language, and I truly look forward to the day when I can say them with pride." Give me a break.

Then, it just hit me – I'd been had! My theory? Somehow the Big Brother who monitors the traffic on match.com figured out I was about to cancel my membership and sent me a reason to stay – Jacques880. There was no way this guy actually existed. And to further investigate my theory, I've talked to a few other women who were about to leave match.com behind. One guess who they all heard from? Yep, Jacques880.

And what about Nick? The guy who started this whole damn thing. After being dumped by Miss Right, Nick was about to cancel his membership on match.com and guess who emailed him? Ding, ding, ding. Yep, Jacques880. Match.com red flag #3.

Dude Looks Like a Lady
Steve Tries Gay Online Dating

If you think straight people have some unbelievable online dating stories, wait until your hear what it's like for a gay man. Our friend Steve is in his early 40's and doesn't come off gay when you first meet him. He's tall, burly, bearded and from the South. Handsome, funny and the nicest guy you'd ever meet, if Steve was straight, Robin would be married to him and we wouldn't have written this book. Living in the West Hollywood area of Los Angeles, Steve got tired of dating "WeHo" boys – extremely good looking, buff, pretty boys from West Hollywood who were only out for an immediate hook-up. So gaycupid.com got a new member.

Steve had only just listed his profile when he got an email from Rick whose tagline read "prince seeking prince." Rick was in his mid-40's, tall, fit and attractive. Not bad for Steve's first encounter. He emailed Rick back and before long, they developed a nice repoire. Rick lived in Seattle and came to L.A. for one week of every month to direct commercials, which he was quite successful at doing. For Steve, this sounded like the perfect intro to a serious relationship. They made plans to meet at the hotel bar of The Standard the next time Rick was in town.

When Steve arrived at the bar, he was not disappointed at all. Rick was even better looking than his photo, very articulate and easy to be around. For those of you new to the gay dating lifestyle, gay men have no problem meeting once, having a drink and hooking up instantly. We'd be lying if we said Steve held out to get to know Rick a little better, so needless to say, they had a great night. The difference here is that both men wanted to see each other again. After Rick went back to Seattle, they stayed in touch and spoke on a regular basis. We saw Steve shortly after that and he was already talking about the things he'd love about living in Seattle – the Space Needle, the coffee, and even the rain. This was a side of Steve we did not see often. God, maybe we should be gay men. So much fucking easier... Anyway, before Steve realized it, Rick was already back in town for his next job.

They met for dinner the first night Rick was back and things picked up right where they left off. Steve had a great time and was even more excited about this guy than before. For their next night, Rick said he had something special planned and hoped Steve had a sense of adventure. Steve started picturing a beautiful hot air balloon ride over the California vineyards or a quick getaway to Vegas to see Celine Dion in concert. Steve took a little extra time getting ready for his date that night as he eagerly awaited Rick's surprise.

When the door of Room 1014 opened, Steve's jaw hit the floor. There stood Rick or should we call him Rita? Rick was wearing a pair of tight Daisy Duke denim shorts, platform

Espadrille shoes and a little half shirt tied in a knot to show off his six pack. To top off this ensemble, Rick finished off the outfit with a pink babushka wrapped around his head and a face of flawless make-up. Estee Lauder would have been proud. Once Steve regained composure, he tried to rationalize the situation. So Rick was into cross-dressing – there were worse things. And, he did look pretty. It wasn't that bad. Steve decided he could deal with it. Poor delusional Steve. Little did he know this was just the tip of the iceberg.

Rick offered him a drink and started behaving like the "woman of the house." It was as if he was June Cleaver entertaining one of Ward's friends. That is until he put on some entertainment in the form of "Chicks with Dicks: The Movie." We weren't watching "Leave it to Beaver" anymore, kids. After he offered Steve some recreational reading material like Buttman magazine, Steve realized this was a situation where he was not comfortable. However, Rick seemed genuinely excited to share this part of him with Steve, so Steve didn't want to be rude and decided to stick it out. Things started to heat up quickly, and Steve thought the sooner he got Rick out of those clothes, the easier this would be... because if Steve wanted to date someone who looked like a woman, he wouldn't be gay. Hello?

First he removed the babushka. Jesus, it made him look like Steve's Aunt Mary. That was better. Then Rick kicked off the Espadrilles – cool, another step to looking like a dude again. But when Steve went for the knotted shirt, Rick made one request: "Can we leave the bra on?" The bra? WTF? Hell no! Steve had to remove the bra. In case you didn't get the memo, gay guys aren't good with bras. Um, that's why they're gay. Steve bit the bullet and when he finally got the damn thing off, he discovered Rick was wearing those "chicken cutlets" that actresses and models wear to increase their bra size. Holy crap, he had "boobies."

In the most feminine voice Rick could muster (think Bea Arthur), he seductively whispered to Steve: "If you treat me like a lady, I'll fuck you like a man." Now we're sure you're thinking Steve got the hell out of dodge. Nope, he's gay. Had sex with him anyway.

Steve got through the sex as best he could and knew this would be the last time he saw Rick. When Rick went back to Seattle, Steve never expected to hear from him again given how awkward that last night had been. Nope, wrong again, Steve. Rick was hooked. He wanted Steve to be his regular "guy" when he was in L.A. So he called Steve one day while running errands. Running errands? What was he buying? Nail polish? Victoria's Secret bra? Tampons? He told Steve he really liked him and he had to be totally honest with him. What could Rick possibly tell him now that wasn't already revealed? Oh no, what if he was already in the process of becoming a woman for real? Like with hormones and surgery and the removal of the one part of his body that gay men really needed? Well, what Rick had to say was far worse than anything Steve was thinking because Rick was apparently running those errands for his wife and two sons. Yep, you read that correctly – WIFE and two SONS. Steve was dumbstruck. This guy was straight? And married to a real woman? Who, according to Rick, actually liked to help him play dress up, but was getting a little bored at the moment. But no, she did not know of Rick's "extra curricular" male activities.

This was all too much for Steve to digest and he told Rick to move on. Rick tried several more times to contact Steve and the last message he left was that he was at a ski resort with his family for their annual vacation. Steve had no trouble picturing Rick busting out a pale pink snowsuit with a matching pom-pom hat that would make even Suzy Chapstick proud.

From Russia With Love
Janet Dates a KGB Spy or Does She?

Janet was a pretty, but ditzy 31-year-old publicity executive who couldn't seem to meet the right guys in L.A. She signed up for Jdate where she met Beck, a tall, handsome 35-year-old professional with jet black curly hair and a great smile. He immediately responded to Janet's email and after a few phone conversations, they went on their first date.

She was impressed when Beck suggested Jones in West Hollywood, a trendy restaurant with a lot of ambience. He asked her if she drank vodka, and when she said yes, he ordered a bottle of the top of line Stolichnaya and an appetizer of their best caviar. Janet was bowled over. She learned he was an internet financier, but deep in his heart, his dream was to be an actor. Oh no. Janet really did not want to date a wannabe actor, but on the plus side, he did have an actor's super good looks and at least he wasn't a waiter. She could live with it. After finishing the bottle of vodka, Beck and Janet engaged in what can only be described as a heavy duty make-out session. You know, the kind where other people are looking at you like "get a room puhleez!"

When they finally came up for air, Beck said he wanted to see her again. Unfortunately, Janet was leaving the next day for Fort Lauderdale to meet her family for a four day vacation. Well, what a co-inky-dink... Beck was also going to be in Fort Lauderdale the day after she arrived. Janet couldn't believe her luck, so they decided to meet up in Florida for their second date. How romantic was that?

So they met in Florida and spent the night hopping from bar to bar on the infamous Fort Lauderdale strip. They ended up on the beach in yet another heavy duty make-out session. At the rate they were going, Janet was going to have to buy more Kiehls Lip Therapy Balm. As they walked to the car, Beck asked her out for a third date once Janet got back to L.A. Unfortunately, when Janet returned, she had to head to Las Vegas for a business trip. She was overseeing the press room for one of Vegas' biggest television conventions. Guess what? Beck said he was also going to be in Vegas at the same time. Hmm, how funny was that? Co-inky-dink number two. Was he going for the television convention? No, he had some meetings of his own set up and didn't elaborate. And the only thing that ran through Janet's mind was three dates in three different states – wow! What ran through our heads wasn't even close to "wow."

During her first night in Vegas, Janet hit the blackjack tables in Mandalay Bay where she was staying and expected to meet up with Beck the next day. Imagine her surprise when she felt a tap on her shoulder to find Beck standing behind her with his luggage in tow. Although she was excited to see him, she knew she heard him correctly when he said he'd be arriving the next day. "Change of plans" was all Beck offered in way of explanation and then asked her to go to dinner. Janet asked if he wanted to check-in first, but he was so happy to see her that all he wanted to do was leave his bags in her room and take care of it later.

That was good enough for Janet and they made their way to the popular Russian restaurant Red Square. When they sat at the bar to wait for their table, Beck started speaking fluent Russian to the bartender as they discussed the 150 vodkas Red Square carried. Say what? RUSSIAN? Where the fuck did this guy learn to speak Russian? There wasn't even a hint of an accent when he spoke.

Once they were seated for dinner, Janet couldn't wait to ask.

Janet: *How do you know how to speak Russian?*
Beck: *I can't say.*
Janet: *Seriously, how do you know how to speak Russian? Were you born there? Your parents? Did you take a Berlitz class for the hell of it?*
Beck: *I can't say.*
Janet: *Beck, seriously, tell me how you know how to speak Russian. It's not like you whipped out a little Spanish here and there. That was full blown Back in the USSR, Cold War, mother fucking Russian.*
Beck: *Ok, I'll tell you.* (Hesitates and then lowers his voice to barely a whisper.) *I am a spy for an underground Russian agency.*

At that point, Janet spit her Siberian nachos across the room.

Janet: *Come the fuck on! What do you think I am? Some kind of idiot? Russian spy my ass. Internet financier by day. Russian spy when? On the weekends?*

Beck: *Janet, I'm very serious about this.*
Janet: *Do you work for the KGB? Are you spying on my country? Are you selling nuclear war secrets?*
Beck: I *can't tell you anymore because if I did, I'd have to kill you. I've already told you too much and put myself in jeopardy.*

At this point, Janet looked around the restaurant for the Punk'd cameras. No producers. No Ashton. And no Boris Yeltsin either. So you would think by now, Janet would be looking for a way out. Nyet. She finished those nachos, the chicken kiev and the bottle of vodka that came with it. She tried several times over dinner to ask him questions, but Beck wouldn't give up anything. So she decided to play it cool until she could get his stuff out of her room and say poka (that's Russian for goodbye.)

Well, things didn't go quite according to plan because Janet, not being the sharpest tool in the box, ended up getting drunk with The Spy Who Loved Me and let him crash in her room. Thankfully she was smart enough to put him fully clothed on the loveseat while she slept alone in the bed with one eye open.

The next morning Janet woke early to get ready for her convention and when she saw him sleeping peacefully on the couch, he looked too cute for her to disturb. Jesus, Janet. She didn't have anything of value in her room anyway, so she gently woke him to tell him he should check into his own room while she went to work. He agreed, said he would take a shower and call her later. She was running late, so she grabbed her laptop and left the room.

When Janet got to the press room, she immediately googled Beck Stevenson and surprisingly, several hits appeared. All of them identified him as an actor with headshot photos, but no mention of any credits and certainly no mention of him being a Russian spy. Well, no shit, Sherlock.

As the end of her work day was approaching, Natasha, oops, we mean Janet, got a call from Beck asking her to go to dinner. Figuring he had gotten his own room by now, she thought it would be safe to have just one more dinner with him. We know what you're thinking – "Janet is a moron." Yes, we know. When she got back to her room, she literally tripped over his luggage which was still sitting on the floor. Hmmm, this is nyet good. But da, Janet finally had a smart thought. She could take this opportunity to turn into the Kremlin and do some KGB spying herself by looking through Beck's stuff. What would turn up? Surveillance equipment? Disappearing ink? A decoder ring?

No, what she did find were several headshot photos of Beck in different poses. Digging deeper, she also found THREE different sets of business cards from THREE different companies with THREE different names. Beck Stevenson, Barry Simon and Bob Sugarman – there was no Vladimir, Yuri or Mikhail among them. Big surprise. Did she not notice that each of those names had the initials "B.S."? As in "bullshit"? Get it, Janet? "B.S."? Crap, this guy was a full fledged scam artist.

All of a sudden there was a knock on the door. It was Beck. Not wanting to be shipped to Siberia, Natasha, um, we mean Janet put everything back in its place. And then she had a thought, if he really was a spy, he would know that she was snooping. Way to go, Janet. The brain cells were working. Beck was cheerful as he entered the room and asked her where she wanted to have dinner. Janet again told him he should check into his own room, but Beck deflected saying he had plenty of time. She explained she had a client dinner that night, so she couldn't meet him. No worries for Beck, he'd just head down to a poker tournament. Damn, this guy just would not leave. Nyet good, people. Nyet good.

Later that night after her dinner, Janet sat down at a blackjack table when who should appear? The Russkie was back. Somehow he had found her randomly in the casino. Was that the first skill they teach in Spy 101 class? He told her he had bought into an all-night poker tournament which was starting shortly, so he'd be out for the whole night. Da! As soon as she heard that, she went straight to the room to collect his luggage. She brought it down to the bellman and said someone named Beck, Barry or Bob might come looking for this and regardless of what name he used, just give him the bags.

Finally, Janet's brain kicked into gear and she became Stalin, Lenin and Khrushchev all in one. She went to the front desk to change rooms and even checked in under a different name. Once inside, she cracked open the mini-bar, pulled out a tiny bottle of Stolichnaya and downed it in one gulp. A toast to you, Beck, Barry, Bob – whatever the fuck your name is. Na pososhok! (Um, that's Russian for "one for the road.)

P.S. She never saw or heard from Beck again. Da.

Hide the Salami
Lauren Meets a New Match.com "Member"

Lauren is a fun-loving, vivacious, 28-year-old from Texas who lived in L.A. She's a party girl who likes to have a good time, but was in a serious relationship for almost four years when her boyfriend woke up one morning, told her he didn't love her anymore and abruptly moved out. After a couple of months of hanging out with Jack Daniels, Jose Cuervo and Jim Beam, Lauren was ready to find a new boyfriend. Match.com got another $39.99. Sigh.

Once she posted her photo, Lauren became a busy girl. She's awfully cute, so she didn't have any problems getting dates, but she was looking for more. She was hoping for romance and found it with Nigel, a charming 38-year-old Englishman who was working in the United States producing commercials for overseas businesses. After a few very eloquent emails, Nigel called Lauren. By their third conversation, Lauren was hooked. His accent was real, he used adorable expressions like "are you being cheeky with me?" and "that's brilliant," played soccer, drank Guinness and watched the BBC. Lauren had found her very own Hugh Grant.

Unfortunately, the timing was bad because Nigel had to travel for a month for his work. They exchanged their real email addresses so they wouldn't need match.com anymore. Fuck off, match.com! Watch out Lauren, Jacques880 is coming.

Everyday Lauren was greeted with a "good morning beautiful" message and every night, he'd tuck her in with a "sweet dreams" email. And for the few times they actually spoke, they had great conversations about art, wine, food, films, music, etc. With each new place he traveled, Nigel would take his laptop and the first thing he did before unpacking, was e-mail Lauren. She got messages from Tokyo, Budapest, Barcelona, Istanbul, London, and it was always something wonderful that sounded like it came straight out of a romance novel.

> "I could not think of a more stunning sight than to walk down the beach with you, to see you framed against the setting sun, in the perfect light with the sea breeze kissing your skin and in your hair and the soft sand between your toes... as the light of the day disappears beyond the horizon... it could only evocate such powerful sense of wanting to feel your body next to mine... I take your hand and lead you to the hotel, to our room overlooking the sea, pour you a glass of wine and for the first time under the crackling light of the fireplace feel your embrace as I softly kiss you into the night."

Now reader, we knew his emails sounded full of shit and Nigel had to be a 45-year-old out-of-work actor who was practicing his accent or a 21-year-old frat boy copying poetry from his English lit text book, but Lauren was convinced he was the real deal. She finally started to feel good again and we didn't want to ruin that for her.

So the romantic e-mails continued back and forth – Lauren felt like the star of her very own Harlequin romance novel. He'd listen to her problems and offer advice, he'd tell her she was beautiful, talk about the romantic scenarios he wanted to create for them and about the gorgeous house he just bought in Santa Barbara. He was very involved in decorating his house and told her about the architecture, the imported furniture and the artwork he was hanging on the walls. At this point, Stacey thought he was cultured and Robin thought he was gay. It all seemed too good to be true. Lauren was giddy and we were suspicious. We asked to see his photo and that's when Lauren said she didn't have one. And she didn't have one because she had never seen what he looked like. What you talking about, Willis? She'd been emailing this guy for over a month and didn't have a clue as to what he looked like? She told us she asked for his photo a few times, but he hadn't found the right one to send her.

Before long, Nigel returned to L.A. and immediately called Lauren to set up their first date. Lauren definitely wanted to meet him, but told Nigel it wasn't fair that he knew what she looked like, but she didn't know what he looked like. She wouldn't go until he sent her a photo. Truthfully, she genuinely liked this guy and it almost didn't matter what he looked like, but still she was curious. Nigel agreed and told her to check her email the next day.

Because we gave her so much shit, Lauren invited us over for the unveiling of Nigel. She eagerly logged on to her computer and saw his email which read: Photo of me while I'm thinking of you, darling. This was it! This was the moment we'd all been waiting for. Was it a photo of him by the Eiffel Tower while he was in Paris? Or maybe by the Taj Mahal while he worked on that shoot in India? The attachment finally downloaded and Lauren felt the butterflies build in her stomach. What if he looked like David Beckham? Robin imagined that he looked like Elton John circa 1987. Stacey hoped for Paul McCartney. As the mouse clicked the attachment, we gathered close to the computer and when the photo opened, three tough broads, one from Brooklyn, one from Staten Island and one from Texas, were rendered speechless. In the attachment, there was a photo of a fully engorged, bright red, uncircumcised, wrinkly, penis with the fattest, saggiest balls any of us had ever seen. Well, top of the morning to you, Nigel.

Nigel not only sent photos, he also gave Lauren his measurements and described how he "thought of her every morning and every night and sometimes even during the day." At this point, Lauren realized she had been duped and it didn't matter where he was from, he was just a perv with saggy balls. Nigel continued to email her until Lauren finally just thanked him for the photos but saggy balls just weren't her cup of tea. So tally ho and cheerio. The three of us hit Fox and Hounds, a British pub in the Valley, where we thoroughly enjoyed a plate of bangers and mash.... without the saggy balls.

Feets Don't Fail Me Now
Alexandra Meets Manola Blahnik

Let's introduce you now to Alexandra – late 30's, very pretty blonde with a toned body, a little shy, reserved and a heart of gold. She and Robin had been working together for the past nine years, but Alex was extremely private. There wasn't too much Alex talked about in the office. So after a devastating break-up with her boyfriend of four years, Alex decided to try online dating. Even though it went against her internet paranoia, and with a lot of coaxing from Robin, Alex signed up for match.com. Sigh, again with the match.com.

After she spent three months getting winked at and emailed by pervy-looking, toothless, gray-haired men old enough to be her grandfather, Alex received an email from Liam, a 38-year-old teacher who looked hot enough to be a Guess model. Immediately suspicious, Robin ran to the computer and we're happy to say it wasn't Jacques880. This guy literally could have been on Sunset Blvd. billboards. He had four photos posted and each one was better than the last – a really good sign. Hells yes, Alex!

They started a nice email exchange – awesome email chemistry was always a great beginning. Their emails led to pleasant phone conversations and soon enough, a date was planned. Alex was excited and nervous! Here she was going on a date with a hot guy with movie star looks and a very humble and giving job. They decided to meet at a neighborhood Irish pub – with a name like Liam, he should be right at home in a pub, right? Just before she left, Alex decided to re-read his profile so she would be prepared for her date with the Irish George Clooney.

Here's what she saw:

- 38-year-old man
- North Hollywood, California, United States
- seeking women 33-40
- within 50 miles of North Hollywood, California, United States

Relationships:	Never Married
Have kids:	None
Want kids:	Yes (2)
Ethnicity:	White / Caucasian
Body type:	Fit/Athletic
Height:	6'3" (190cms)
Religion:	Religious
Smoke:	No Way
Drink:	Social drinker, maybe one or two

Yep, so far so good. She continued on to his introductory paragraph:

> I'm a down to earth, honest, hard working guy looking for that one special woman to complete me. She should enjoy candlelight dinners, long walks on the beach and the occasional trip to an amusement park – sorry, I'm kid at heart! I'm looking for an athletic girl who's comfortable in jeans or formal dress and can kick up her heels in fancy shoes and have a good time.

Alex could kick up her heels with the best of them. So as she waited in the pub for her Irish Clooney to arrive, she envisioned their first vacation together to Ireland to visit the Blarney Stone. When she felt a tap on her shoulder, her stomach filled with butterflies in anticipation of seeing Liam in person, but when she turned around, she was staring straight into the face of what could only be described as Liam's grandfather. This dude was old! She realized the pictures on his profile had to be about 15 years old or they were really artfully photo shopped. Even though his face was handsome, he had more wrinkles than her neighbor's Sharpei. Being the mature, open-minded and painfully single woman she was, Alex decided not to be superficial because it's what is on the inside that really counts. And hey, dating an older man could be a new and good experience. Ok, but just how old was he?

As he sat in the booth and ordered his beer, she was acutely aware that the atmosphere between them was tense. Alex thought he might be nervous because he kept dropping things on the floor. First it was the silverware. Then it was the napkin. The third time, it was his cell phone. The last time he bent over to reach underneath the table to retrieve an item, Alex decided to try to break the ice:

Alex: *So, with a name like Liam, you must have a very rich Irish ancestry.*
Liam (with a blank look on his face): *No, actually my parents are Hispanic.*

Blink, blink. Blink, blink. What? Hispanic? How many Hispanic Liams did you know?

Alex: *So being Hispanic, how did you end up with a name like Liam?*
Liam: *Don't know, my parents are dead.*

Really deep breath. Here we go again, one more try.

Alex: *Ok, so you're a teacher. That has to be a very rewarding profession. What do you teach?*
Liam: *Traffic school.*

Big sigh. All righty then. They finished their beer in a very awkward silence and it was apparent this date was over. As they left the pub, Liam or Jose or Miguel or whatever the fuck his name was insisted on walking Alex to her car. Since this was a gentlemanly gesture, she let him.

Once they left the pub, Senor Liam came alive. His demeanor lightened up and he started getting quite talkative. He asked some basic questions about her life and job until they arrived at her car.

Alex (clearly wanting to end the date): *So thanks for a nice evening. Here's my car – guess I'll go now.*
Liam: *Can I ask you something? How many pairs of shoes do you own?*

Alex: *Uh, excuse me? I don't know.*
Liam: *I'm curious. Do you have 50 pairs of shoes?*
Alex: *50 pairs? That's a lot of shoes – probably not.*
Liam: *Well, do you have at least 20 pairs of shoes?*

Wait a minute, was this guy serious? Oh yeah, he was dead serious.

Liam: *I'm fascinated by women's shoes.*
Alex: *Oh, are you an aspiring designer?*
Liam: *No. How many pairs of pumps do you have? Sandals? Open toe? Red shoes? Boots? Oh yeah, boots. I like boots. You know, there's a DSW around the corner. What do you say we continue our date there and I buy you a pair of shoes?*

At that moment, Alex flashed back to his profile – "hoping to meet an athletic girl who can kick up her heels in fancy shoes." And when he asked what kind of shoes she was wearing that night, it dawned on her that the reason he kept dropping things under the table was to look at her feet. Holy crap! This guy was a freak. A really old looking, wannabe Irish, foot fetish creep. As Alex clicked the alarm on her car, she desperately looked around for anyone who could help her if she needed it. Jimmy Choo? Manola Blahnik? Guy who owns Payless? Anyone? There was no one, so she opted to play it cool with her weird muchacho until she could get into her car and run for her life.

Just wanting to get away from him, Alex agreed to meet him at DSW. Liam took off for his car faster than you can say Carrie Bradshaw so Alex peeled off and headed home to her small, but fabulous shoe collection. And by the way Liam, she was wearing open-toe gold wedge Christian Loubitains or you probably call them "loubies."

Serial Dating 101
Stacey Scores with Singlesnet.com

As our voyage to find true love online continued, we were shocked at just how many sites there were to find your soul mate. It was pretty amazing. It seemed anyone could find love... even if you were a cross-dresser who adopted stray pets, did origami and only ate green foods... trust us, there was a site for you. While strolling through the vast number of sites, I decided on singlesnet.com.

Why singlesnet.com? Why not. I saw signs posted for it and it was one of the first sites that came up on a search. And it was so easy. Barely any application to fill out and very straightforward. This was who I am and what I wanted. After the 72 hours I put into eHarmony only to get my latest match – Dexter the bookbinder from British Columbia – singlesnet.com was a breeze. (BTW, Dr. Warren, British Columbia? Now I'm not matchable in the entire United States?) I posted my profile, sans photo to start, and before I could get through my "welcome to singlesnet.com" email, I had ten "flirts" (the singlesnet.com version of a match.com "wink"). Ten "flirts"? All in the United States? And in the

Los Angeles area? Thank God. Maybe I wouldn't die alone and unmatchable now.

Ok, before you get too excited, not every "flirt" and email I received was marrying material. Or even dating material for that matter. Word of advice gentlemen: choosing a screenname is really important. Really, really important – and I'm talking to you sircumsalot, longtongue4u69, Tantricsx4ever, 9inchesplus, marriedsowhat, and dickycocknuts who were just a few of the men I deleted instantly. The good thing I noticed about singlesnet.com was when I flirted, men flirted back right away. The bad thing was, well, when I looked at dickycocknuts to see what kind of moron posted that profile, dickycocknuts could see I looked at him. Ah Christ... then I couldn't lose the guy. "Hey, thanks for checking out my profile – guess you liked what dickycocknuts has to offer, huh?" Oh for fuck's sake.

So I weeded out the crap, narrowed down the "flirts" and emails I liked, sent a few myself and waited for the games to begin. And did they begin! Before the end of my first week on singlesnet.com, I had five dates set up, three offers for a one night stand, two marriage proposals (from russianman4u and lovemeandmycats) and one man from Ghana who only needed $2,000 to help his sick mother return to the country. Not bad for one week and this was before I even posted my photo. Once I did that, the floodgates opened. Hallelujah, it was raining men.

Before I knew it, I couldn't keep track of who I was going out with, who I'd been talking to and who I emailed with on a regular basis. And then dozens more flirts and emails would come in a 24-hour period. Keep in mind, there was lots of weeding going on, but there were some good men on singlesnet.com. So after I made my spreadsheet and updated my chart to keep things in order, I started dating... and dating...and dating. There were times I had three dates a week or would be making dates with guys on the way to a date with another guy. It was almost impossible to keep track of everyone. Obviously, I didn't click with them all, but they were all pretty much pleasant experiences. No freaks, all employed, all attractive, some who are still friends to this day and some whom I wanted to fix up with other friends.

Now, I'd be lying if I didn't mention one negative experience by the name of Tim – or Italy512. We spoke for weeks and finally made plans to meet at a cool Mexican place located close to his house and my job. I texted him when I got to the restaurant at 7pm to let him know where I was sitting. No text back. Hmm, well, maybe he was driving and couldn't respond. 7:15pm, sent another text making sure he remembered. 7:30pm, called him and left a message on his voicemail. That's when I started to get a bad feeling about it. 7:45pm, I was done. Fucking loser. I called a friend who was still at work to meet me for dinner and we had a great time. As we were leaving the restaurant, my phone rang and we both eagerly looked at the caller ID expecting it to be Tim with some lame excuse but instead it was Brian. Jackpot! He was the one on singlesnet I'd been hoping would call all along. Suck it, Tim!

Brian was a 36-year-old videographer and editor. He was 6'1, brown hair, hazel eyes and kind of reminded me of Brendan Fraser. Not bad, right? When I got my first email from him, it was cute and articulate and his picture was adorable. He left me his phone number right away and I couldn't dial it fast enough. Our first conversation lasted over an hour and to be honest, I was hooked. God, I really hoped this guy called again. And he just did.

In the meantime, I couldn't put all of my eggs in the Brian basket, so over a two month period of time, I dated a number of good guys. Thankfully, Brian was one of them. There was Sean the actor and massage therapist. We went out a bunch of times and had fun, but ended up better as friends and still talk today. John the catering manager and Jersey boy. Really cool guy, but not a love connection. Erik the lighting tech for a chain of clubs. Nice guy, good date but no chemistry. Jeff the culinary student. Can't say enough good things about Jeff. He's the kind of guy you marry, but Brian was still leading the pack and I didn't want to lead Jeff on. So ladies, go find him!

While this sounds like it was a lot of fun, and it was, I was tired. So many first dates, so little time. But no matter whom I went out with, my thoughts always went back to Brian. He was really busy with his job and family and just struggling to keep his life together so we didn't see much of each other, although we spoke very frequently. I definitely liked this guy. After our third date, he told me he was already starting to think of me as his girlfriend and wanted to try dating exclusively to see where it would go. Back in the day, this would seem a little on the quick side, but in the world of online dating we'd known each other a lifetime. Three dates in the real world equals a year in the online world. Believe me, this was rare and exciting. I challenged Brian to take down his profile to see if he was serious... and he did. That meant I had to do the same... to be continued!

Match.com is Still (and Always Will Be) Full of Shit - Allegedly
Robin's Rant

The plan for this chapter was to write about our friend Joe, but Robin left the notes about his story at the office. So while Stacey started to rant about wasting the writing time, Robin started to rant about the anti-Christ... a.k.a. match.com. And guess what? A new chapter was born.

I had been on match.com since November 2007. And despite Stacey's fake romance with Jacques, I was still plugging away as were several of my friends who ranged in age from 28 to 48 and while all very pretty, all looked very different. There was something for everyone depending on taste. Somehow each of us was having the same complaint about the site. We would wink at multiple guys and never get a response until we were ready to cancel our memberships. Hmmm....

After God knows how many "winks," I finally connected with a match.com guy and we went on our first date. Mike was a 37-year-old fifth grade teacher who loved 80's metal bands and the famous Rainbow restaurant – my two favorite things in life. He was a good looking guy with a very noble profession and I was looking forward to a nice evening. And surprise! I did have a nice evening. Our date lasted four hours and we had a lot in common. I definitely wanted to go out with him again. Lo and behold, the second date curse was broken because Mike asked me out for the following week. Yee haw!

After chatting on the phone throughout the week leading up to date night, Mike asked me to meet him at his apartment so we could drive to the restaurant together. I wasn't comfortable going to his house, so I suggested we meet at the restaurant. I guessed that must've pissed him off because the guy I went out with that night was not the same guy I went out with the week before. He was boring, rude and overall lethargic. WTF? He kept talking about his female friend Christine who taught kindergarten and who was his "buddy." They went to concerts together, took trips together, painted each other's nails, blah, blah, blah. Well, if she was so friggin wonderful, then why wasn't she sitting across from him at this craphole of a restaurant which he raved about all week? Little aside – it was called Casablanca because it was themed after the movie. However, they served Mexican food... really bad Mexican food. And their specialty? Squid. Squid?? Are Mexicans known for their squid? The last time I watched Casablanca, Humphrey Bogart was not chowing down on a chile relleno with squid. But I digress.

The date was so bad, I mentally checked out and started to analyze the couples eating dinner around me. There was the guy at the next table who looked like my loser ex; there was a gay couple who were so in love, I wanted to vomit; and there was a 350 pound Mexican woman making out with her 92 pound boyfriend while I'm sitting across from a man who must have smoked twenty joints before coming to meet me. I'M GOING TO DIE ALONE.

After graciously offering to split the bill with me, we left the restaurant and Mike quickly said "let's call it a night." Fine with me, bucko. You suck anyway. That was my last thought as he got in his car and drove away leaving me to walk two blocks in the dark by myself in a sketchy neighborhood in order to get to my car. Parents beware: if Mike is one of your children's teachers, I'd think twice before letting him chaperone any class trips. Your kids might have to find their own way home. Unless, of course, Fraulein Christine is on the bus. And that was the moment I decided to cancel my match.com subscription.

Was there anyone out there who can attest to what goes on inside the match.com machine? Was the great and powerful Wizard with a Magic Eight Ball controlling the entire site? Was it a 25th century self-sufficient computer that will eventually take over the world? Or was everything routed to East India where a bunch of non-English speaking 11-year-olds were paid .25 a day to handle all of the emails and "winks"? Any and all of these explanations might shed some light on why this site sucks my ass. As Stacey mentioned earlier, there was a pattern on this site that within two weeks of canceling your membership, Ryan Reynolds, Jake Gyllenhall and Jon Bon Jovi suddenly appear in your inbox. The same thing happened to each of us as we were getting ready to cancel – an email from the most perfect man in the world arrived and we extended our membership for another three months in order to converse with him. And then Mr. Perfect disappeared.

In my case, I started to explore other websites while I waited for match.com to expire when out of the blue, Tom and Ron contacted me. Tom was 6'2 with piercing blue eyes and jet black hair. I almost orgasmed looking at his picture. Ron, while not my type, was Mr. Attractive All American. And I wanted to go out with both of them. I emailed them back and both of them asked for my phone number. Woo hoo! Stacey never got past Jacques' eloquent belletristic prose, so maybe these guys were actually real if they asked to call me.

Two days later, I received a voicemail from Tom who had the sexist voice I'd ever heard. I saved it and lulled myself to sleep with it every night. Ron, who lived in Las Vegas but was going to be in L.A. for the weekend, called to set up a date. I had hit the motherlode. When I tried to call Tom back, I realized he didn't leave a number nor did his number did not come up on my called ID because it was private. But Ron and I spoke and we made plans to meet for lunch on the Sunday before he left to go back to Vegas.

Well, dear reader, guess what? Tom is M.I.A – never to be heard from again. People, check the back of milk cartons. And at 2pm on the day of my date with Ron, I was sitting in Stacey's house writing this chapter because he never showed up. I haven't been stood up since the 7th fucking grade. Match.com, you are going to burn in hell. It's time to come clean, you mofos, because we all know neither Tom nor Ron were real - *allegedly*. I had no doubt they both were *allegedly* match.com decoys so I would renew my membership. But ha! I'm on to you... as is Alex, Keri, Lauren, Jennifer, Nick and Stacey who started the whole expose into the bullshit that is match.com. As a matter of fact, when we googled match.com, a number of stories came up about online daters suing the site for fraud. One article, which appeared in USA Today, reports on a federal lawsuit filed against the site for goading members into renewing memberships though bogus romantic emails. Now, since we don't want to piss off the powers that be at match.com because they have enough money to run a new commercial every thirty seconds, we will be clear in saying the above is our personal experience and those of people who told us first hand. We and the people who filed those lawsuits are *curious* about the alleged fake emails we've received when we were getting near cancellation. That's all we're saying, people. Seems peculiar. We're sure there are people who have found love on match. But if you haven't and you're looking for an interesting read, do a little web search and see what comes up.

In the meantime, I found a new site called plentyoffish.com. Of course, I'd only joined it for the good of this book (Stacey: *sure you did.*) So I picked up my bait, cast my reel and if anyone was looking for me, I'd gone fishing.

I'm a Slave For You
Steve's Icing on the Cake

In the gay world, there are categories to represent how gay men describe themselves. In Steve's case, he's considered a "bear," so it was only natural that he went to a site called bear411.com to find his next online love. He was only on the site for a few weeks and had some casual encounters before he met Lucques, a French pastry chef from Pasadena. In his mid-30's, Lucques was a nice looking guy and after a short exchange of emails and phone calls, seemed really into Steve. And vice versa. This guy might be worth putting in some time. And it didn't hurt that every morning, Steve envisioned waking up to fresh croissants, chocolate éclairs, baguettes and endless cups of café au lait. While getting ready for his date, Steve wondered if Lucques wore those big, white pastry chef hats and used an icing gun when he made cream puffs. Or maybe he looked like the guy from "Ace of Cakes." Either way, it was all good.

They decided to meet at the Chateau Marmont for aperitifs (get used to it reader, we're milking this.) Steve had barely taken his first sip when Lucques laid it all out on the table for him – he told Steve that was looking to be someone's slave. Excuse moi? What kind of slave was Lucques referring to? He was willing to do or be anything Steve wanted. Lucques encouraged Steve to be open-minded and give it a try, so they made plans to meet the following night.

As Steve paced his apartment trying to come up with tasks for his French slave, he was concerned that he didn't have a dungeon or use a Cat o'Nine Tails. He didn't even own a run of the mill ball gag. Really Steve, what kind of gay man are you? As he tripped over a pile of dirty laundry on his bedroom floor and made his way into the bathroom where the soap scum was an inch think on the sink, a light bulb went off in Steve's head. Voila! He knew exactly what to ask for from his first rendezvous with Lucques.

Lucques arrived on time and raring to go. He told Steve he was sexually charged up about this night and anything Steve wanted to do would be fine with him – he could put a leash on him and drag him around or he would wear a butt plug and ball gag (no can do, Steve doesn't own one, Lucques.) Basically, anything goes. Bon vivant! So here's how it happened:

Steve: *Bon jour, Lucques. I'd like you to undress and put on this jock.*
Lucques: *Oh yes, that sounds hot.*
Steve: *Then I want you to pick up that feather duster…*
Lucques (heavy breathing): *And? And put it where?*
Steve: *In your right hand…*
Lucques (starting to sweat): *What else, master?*
Steve: *No, call me Monsieur.*

Lucques: *Oui, Monsieur. Anything you ask.*
Steve: *Follow me into the bedroom.*
Lucques (jock strap rising): *Oui.*
Steve (pointing to the clothing on the floor): *As my slave, what I really want you to do is... clean... my... fucking... apartment.*

And Lucques did just that. He did a really good job, too. So much so, that Steve, being the stand-up guy that he was, let Lucques give him a blow job when he was done. Lucques was such a talented domestic goddess that Steve decided to take advantage of his culinary skills and had him whip up some chocolate mousse before he left. Mental note: next time ask him to bring the pastry hat.

As Steve was licking the last of the mousse out of the bowl and admiring his sparkling home, he knew he would be seeing Lucques again. Lucques was all too happy to accommodate and each time, cleaned the house like a bona fide indentured servant, baked him lot of goodies and used his oral skills well. But after a few weeks, Lucques raised the bar. He wanted Steve to verbally abuse him (you suck, Lucques), spank him for not cleaning the house well enough (eh, but not hard) and asked to lick Steve's feet (Ew, faux pas, Lucques! You just crossed the line there. Steve don't do feet.)

While Steve actually did like Lucques and considered seeing him on a regular basis, the fetish thing freaked him out. On paper, he was the perfect boyfriend – he cooked, he cleaned and he was always up for sex. But in reality, the slave thing was too much for Steve. So au revoir, salut and adieu, Lucques. See you in Robin and Stacey's roman a clef.

So while Steve was still looking for love online, Lucques may be gone but not forgotten because Steve has since hired Merry Maids, a legitimate cleaning service which comes weekly… but without the éclairs. C'est la vie.

Where is Waldo?
Meet Stacey's New Boyfriend

I did it. I found my man. My boyfriend. And I did it online. I made the decision to let Brian be the one. Why waste any more time dating when this guy obviously was really into me and wanted me to be his girlfriend? We were going to be a couple. I would have dates every weekend. Birds were singing, the sun was shining and little bunny rabbits sat at my window. I would have someone to share my ups and downs, good times and bad times. We would laugh together, eat Chinese food in bed together, watch all of the "Jersey Shore" reruns together. I was going to be a Hallmark greeting card.

So now that Brian and I were officially "boyfriend and girlfriend," I was looking forward to spending some quality time with him so we could really get to know each other. I assumed we'd hang out regularly. Wasn't that what couples did? Our phone conversations were so easy, it was as if we were already falling into a pattern – little did I know then that we were falling into a pattern, but not necessarily a good one. We talked about plans and the future, but somehow it always just remained talk. Literally, just talk. It would go something this:

Brian: *"I can't wait to see you this weekend. I know I've been so busy working on editing, trying to book gigs and dealing with my grandfather, but I'm going to clear the whole day on Sunday for us. Sound good?*

Stacey: *"That sounds great. I had plans, but I will change them for you."*

Brian's schedule was so hectic I didn't mind making some compromises. Wasn't this was what you're supposed to do? By the time Friday rolled around, I couldn't wait to leave the office and hook up with Brian.

Friday

Stacey: *"Oh, hey Brian, just leaving you a message to see if you're still ok for Sunday. Let me know – talk to you soon."*

Brian: *Nothing.*

Saturday

Stacey: *"Morning Brian, it's me – just wondering if we're still on for tomorrow. Call or email, text is fine. I'm looking forward to seeing you."*

Brian: *Radio silence.*

Stacey: *"Brian, it's Stacey, around 5pm, calling about tomorrow."*

Hello? Is this thing on? Bueller, Bueller.

So after checking my cell phone 50 times to make sure it was charged and working properly, I then checked my email. Nothing. No response from him in now three days. This from a guy I was talking to several times a day. A guy who called every night to say good night. Of course, that was all before he became my "boyfriend." What the fuck kind of boyfriend was this?

When I didn't hear from him by Sunday morning, I made plans for the day. Robin and I went out for dinner that night and just before I went to bed, my phone rang. Guess who?

Brian: *"Oh, hey it's me, sweetie. Sorry about this weekend – I got caught up at the gig and spent all day working on the photos for the client. Such a pain in the ass..."*

Stacey: *"And you couldn't find five minutes in three days to call your girlfriend to let me know you were canceling?"*

Brian: *"No, sweetie, you don't understand. I left my phone in my coat pocket and I couldn't remember your number to call you cause I didn't have my phone."*

Stacey: *"You left your phone in your pocket for three days?"*

Brian: *"I'm so sorry. I know I'm bad about communicating. I'm gonna make it up to you. Please don't be mad – it won't happen again. I promise! I'm just really excited about you and us and want us to be together."*

Not wanting to start this off as the naggy girlfriend, I let it go and for the next few days, he was fine... on the phone. Although at some point, it occurred to me that he hardly ever answered when I called. I always got his voicemail. Things that make you go hmmm.

Still, he told me to hold that Friday night for him because he was planning a special outing for us. Ok, sounded good. And before long, the week was almost over and I hadn't heard from Brian. I left him a message from work because once again, I got his voicemail. No call back.

On Thursday, I sent him a text. No response. On Friday, the day of our special date, I never heard from him at all. It had been almost a week since we last spoke. WTF? This was some serious bullshit.

It was Saturday afternoon before I heard from him.

Brian: *"Hey sweetie, what's up?*
Stacey: *"Brian, what the fuck?"*
Brian: *"Oh, I'm really sorry about yesterday, but I had to go down to San Diego again for my grandfather. You know how sick he's been and he had problems with the nurse who called a social worker…"*

And as he rambled on and on about his grandfather and how much he had to do for him and how the weight of the world was on his shoulders and how sorry he was about me, etc., all I could think about was how easy it would have been for him to just text me while on his three hour drive to San Diego. Just six little words like, say "grandfather is sick. Going to SD." Was that so hard in the world we live in where your five year old neighbor owned a cell phone, blackberry and iPad? It's not like he had to stop at the only pay phone on the 405.

What to do? What to do? On one hand, my bullshit detector was kicking in and I thought he might be lying. On the other hand, why did he go through all of the trouble to come on so strong and escalate the relationship after only the third date? And on my imaginary third hand, I did really like him and kept hoping he would get it together. So, I decided to give him one last chance.

One month later. Lather, rinse, repeat and repeat and repeat. Just as I predicted, Brian blew me off multiple times with the same lame excuses – work, grandfather, misplaced his phone, etc. Ok, let me break it down for you. I had been his "girlfriend" for a month and I never saw him once. Hello? Once! One time. One date. I saw Robin every week – she could have been my boyfriend.

His job was demanding, but not impossible. He wasn't off saving an African village where they might not get cell phone reception. And he wasn't friggin' Jack Bauer who only had 24 hours to save the world from terrorists. And even Jack Bauer makes time to call his girlfriend. He was an editor in a post house. Last time I checked, there were phones in the edit bay at Sony studios.

By this point, I examined my situation. I wasn't desperate and didn't need to be in a "relationship" with someone who clearly had something else going on. I hated to admit it, but I began thinking that maybe he had ANOTHER girlfriend, or worse… a WIFE! That stupid imaginary third hand.

So I left him a message to call me. After a week, he finally called back. But I wasn't even angry anymore because I no longer cared what he had to say. I was tired of playing his game, so I asked him straight out if he had a girlfriend or a wife… and he paused… just a bit too long. What a douchebag. So I updated my profile, added some new pictures and I was back to online dating. Since I really didn't like any of the other sites, I decided to stick with singlesnet because other than Big Love Brian, I did meet some nice guys. What did I have to lose? However, I wasn't finished with Brian. I wasted my time and my emotions. I was going to get to the bottom of this. And when I did… be afraid, Brian, be very afraid.

It Takes Two to Tango
Shari and the Ferret

Sometimes an online date isn't disastrous because the guy is crazy, or sexually deviant, or secretly married. Sometimes, there just isn't an attraction. What looks good on paper somehow doesn't make the transition.

Shari was a cute, successful, educated Jewish chick who worked in the home entertainment department for a big studio. And by the time she was in her late 20's, Shari was convinced she would die alone. But instead of picking out her tombstone, she decided to join Jdate – just another form of slow death.

After a stream of unsuccessful dates with poor wannabe writers and actors where she found herself often paying the check, she decided to up the requirements of her search and only target men with graduate degrees in paying professions who could at least cover the cost of her non-fat latte at Starbucks. That's when she met Ira, aka The Ferret.

On the plus side, Ira was a graduate of Harvard Law School and a practicing attorney in the Santa Monica area – perfect because that's where she lived. On the down side, he was 5'6"with mousy brown hair, a pointed jaw and a really bony face. Let's face it people, there was no sugar coating this – he looked like a ferret. Again, dear reader, you might be noticing a pattern here, but for many women, it's true...it's what's on the inside that counted. So Shari and Ira started an email exchange. Surprisingly, Ira was funny in his emails and Shari could tell he had a good personality, so they made plans to meet. Ira was really busy during the week due to his successful law practice, so he asked her out for a Saturday night. Ooooh... red flag for Shari. Saturday nights were prime real estate and she was afraid she'd appear desperate if she was available. But Shari looked at the alternative. She was single and planning on sitting on the couch with a bag of Cheetos, watching an episode of SNL, now in its 400th season. So she decided to bite the bullet and agreed to a Saturday night first date.

Ira took his Saturday night date duties very seriously and made reservations at an upscale restaurant which only locals frequented. On the Thursday before the date, he called to tell her the restaurant was known for their seafood – especially their salt-crusted sea bass which usually sold out on a weekend. May he reserve one for her? Well, well. Ira was pulling out all of the stops and Shari was impressed.

Saturday Night

It could not have been a worse night for a first date. Torrential rain storms had hit Los Angeles and for those of you who do not live here, that's the equivalent of living in Buffalo and getting hit with a blizzard. Despite not feeling up to the date, Shari rallied because Ira did pre-order some fish, and went to meet him. He was already waiting for her at the table when she arrived. Ira got up to greet her and Shari was shocked – although she knew what he looked like and had seen his photo, there was no mistaking the resemblance to a ferret up close and in person. He took her jacket and signaled the maitre' de, who immediately exchanged the little display flower on the table for a gi-normous bouquet which Ira had brought with him. These flowers were so big, that when they sat down at the table, Shari couldn't even see Ira sitting across from her.

Shari pushed the Kentucky Derby-sized flower arrangement to the side and did her best to get through the date. Even though there wasn't any physical attraction on her part, she did want to try to get to know him and give it a chance. Ira tried his best to impress her which soon turned into 20 minutes of Ira droning on with stories about law school, working 75 hours a week, how much money he spent on his foreign sports car, and how many women he gets emails from on Jdate. The way Ira was talking, you would think he was a bona fide chick magnet. This pretty much confirmed for Shari there would be no emotional connection either.

When the waiter approached to take their drink order, Shari ordered a glass of house Chardonnay. No, no, no, screamed Ira. He insisted that she have the most expensive wine on the list because he was, after all, a wine connoisseur to boot and he could not watch her drink stuff he considered nothing but Boone's Farm. Ok, let's just sum up the situation so far. Ira was unattractive, boring, full of himself and a snob. And that was all before he laid on her his latest piece of news. Ira had a hidden talent. Are you ready? When he wasn't defending big firms for tax evasion (yawn), nebbishie, ferret faced, little

Ira was a... wait for it. SALSA instructor. No way. Hello? Wasn't a salsa instructor supposed to look like Ricky Martin?

Before Shari could even absorb this new piece of information, her salted fish came and she was glad to have the food to concentrate on, that was until Ira turned the conversation to dating off of Jdate. To her surprise and relief, Ira told her he often went out on dates where there was clearly no connection and the situation would become awkward. Ding, ding, ding! Ira hit the nail on the head! This was one of those dates and Shari was thrilled that he seemed to recognize it as well. Whew! She then began to enjoy her highly demanded salted fish and pretty much tuned him out for the rest of the meal. And by the way, it was good, but not good enough to order three days in advance.

After they finished eating, Shari thought the date was finally over for both of them. But Ira insisted he didn't want the evening to end. Shari was shocked. She thought it was clear to both of them there was no interest. Maybe she was too polite about it because he now wanted to take her ice skating and to the Santa Monica pier to ride the Ferris wheel. And then the dreaded one – he wanted to take her dancing so she could see how he really moved on the dance floor. Wink, wink. What?? No!! They agreed it was awkward, remember? The only place Shari wanted to see Ira move was out of this restaurant and into his car. Not wanting to spend any more time with him, Shari said they could go dancing next time because after all, it was raining. Yes, we know – raining has nothing to do with dancing. But in Los Angeles, rain is an excuse to *not* do almost anything. And because she kept blaming the rain, Ira then insisted he drive her to her car because well, it was raining.

Once in his tiny, two seater car where there was barely enough room for Shari and the flowers, Ira again said he didn't want the date to end. Trapped in the car with the ferret and the flowers, Shari didn't have much of a choice as Ira started to drive away from the restaurant without even asking her where her car was parked. While this could probably be legally constituted as kidnapping, Shari wasn't afraid. She knew she could take him with those damn flowers if he tried anything.

Okay, maybe he was like Patrick Swayze on the dance floor, so she agreed to go, but she had to make sure of one thing - there was no way she would be seen with him in her neighborhood. Now she would see how well Ira could shake it. She suggested a rave club in Hollywood and luckily for them it was 80's night. At least no one Shari knew would see Ira bust out The Robot. We would love to tell you Ira was magic on the dance floor, but then we would be lying. And when Ira started to grind up on her like a dog in heat with a white man's overbite and fists pumped high in the air, Shari felt she had done her part for the fucking overrated salt-crusted sea bass and Sea Biscuit flowers. When the DJ started to spin some Bangles, she was mortified as the crowd watched Ira "Walk Like an Egyptian." Did people really pay him money to learn to dance? Once "Rapper's Delight" came on, Shari broke into a cold sweat in fear that Ira would start break dancing. So before he did the moonwalk, she told him it was time to go and he reluctantly agreed. With nothing to say to each other on the way back and Ira still being all keyed up, he put on the radio and oh no... it was Saturday's 70's Night on 103.5. Big sigh as Ira hustled in the car all the way home.

Thar She Blows
Aaron Meets Old Faithful

Aaron, a 33-year-old, good looking investment banker and one of the nicest guys we know could not find a girlfriend to save his life. Instead of packing it up and moving home to live with his mother, he decided to join americansingles.com. As soon as he posted his profile, he was besieged by eager, pretty, single women from all over Los Angeles. The first girl he started talking to was Michelle, a 32-year-old advertising executive from the Valley. There was instant chemistry between them and for the first time in a long time, Aaron had hopes his dry spell had come to an end.

They made plans to meet at Nic's, a popular martini bar in Beverly Hills. The date was effortless as they hit it off immediately and the conversation flowed easily. By the end of the night, they had already planned the second date. Aaron was beside himself – the heavens opened and the sun was shining – he liked Michelle! He stopped emailing other prospects that night because it was all about Michelle.

For the next date, they went to dinner and a movie. Another great night that didn't end there – she invited him back to her apartment afterwards for a nightcap. One glass of wine later and they were making out or as Aaron puts it, she "face raped him." Say what? Her tongue went places he didn't even know existed on his face. He barely got the chance to kiss her because she licked up, she licked down, side to side – all in all, he felt like a Tootsie Pop.

But the face rape didn't deter Aaron. He still liked Michelle, quirks and all, so they made plans for a third date. After all, if she used her tongue that expertly on his face, oh the places they could go. The next date was dinner at her apartment which she cooked for them and Aaron thought that would be *the* night. Bow chika bow bow. After two bottles of wine and a delicious home cooked meal, things started to heat up quickly. It was only seconds before the tongue made its second appearance and violated Aaron's face almost illegally. She led him into the bedroom and started to undress. Aaron opened his wallet to pull out a condom, when Michelle stopped him:

Michelle: *What are you doing? You don't need to wear a condom with me.*
Aaron: *Uh, yeah I do.*
Michelle: *No, seriously, you don't.*
Aaron: *Uh, seriously, yeah I do.*
Michelle: *Aaron, you don't need to wear a condom because I'm a virgin.*

Um, Houston, we have a problem.

WHAT THE FUCK? A VIRGIN? AT HER AGE? Standing naked in her bedroom on the third date? As Aaron's erection slowly started to fade, Michelle grabbed his hand to lead him to the bed because as she put it, "she did everything but." Aaron was speechless and almost erectionless at this point and didn't know what to do. He hadn't heard that expression since his senior year of high school. How could she still be a virgin? Was this fucking Little House on the Prairie? But she was a face raper, people! Laura fucking Ingalls the face raper with a tongue Gene Simmons would envy. On the other hand, he was in the middle of a pretty big dry spell and any activity now still sounded good to him. So he followed her to the bed despite the huge blaring warning bell ringing in his head.

They started fooling around, and the more excited she became... how should we put this? The more excited she became, the more uh, lubricated she became. Since it was determined that Aaron's penis would not be penetrating any part of Michelle, he decided to visit her downtown. It was like a slip n' slide in there. Just when she was about to reach orgasm, Michelle let out a moan that sounded like a fog horn. Her body started to quake like Moby Dick was rising from the depths of the ocean and before Aaron could even react, Old Faithful had erupted and gushed, and gushed and then gushed some more. The only time he had ever seen anything like this was in a porn movie. He heard women could do this, but didn't really believe it. Poor Aaron's orgasm paled in comparison.

Michelle: *"Wow, that was great."*
Aaron: *"Um... yeah."*
Michelle: *"Do you want to get together again?"*

No, he wanted to say. I want to towel off, get in my car and drive far away from you, you freak of nature. But instead it came out more like this:

Aaron: *"Yes, I do."*

HELLOOOOOO? What was he thinking? He asked himself the same thing on the way home. But he had to admit, he was kind of intrigued. Would she be able to do that again?

When Aaron told us about his aquatic adventure, we were stunned. No way she was still a virgin and no way he had actually met a genuine gusher. Even though Aaron knew the virginity thing would eventually be an issue, he desperately tried to rationalize the situation because he so very much wanted a girlfriend. We quickly pointed out that not only is being a virgin at her age in these times in Los Angeles a strange characteristic, but girls like her will expect him to marry them at the point of penetration. Stay away, far away.

But did Aaron listen? Nah. He went on date number four thinking he would be the stud. Dude, big mistake. Better bring snorkeling gear. They had a great date where they went to a popular sushi and karaoke place called Tidal Wave. No, really. It was called Tidal Wave. For those of you who don't believe us, it's in a strip mall on Sunset and Gower not far from Paramount Studios. During karaoke, she sang a Billy Ocean song followed by a rousing rendition of Under the Boardwalk and closed with It's Raining Men. Ok, we're kidding about the songs.

In the bedroom that night, Aaron soon discovered the first deluge was not a fluke. Michelle really did have a unique happy ending and effusively expressed her total satisfaction with their teenage tryst. Aaron wasn't sure how long he could keep this up – how many times can a guy dip his toe in the water but never go for a swim?

While lying in bed, Aaron asked her why she was still a virgin at her age. Unfazed, Michelle explained the man she had sex with would be the man she married and the father of her children. Sex was sacred to her and the other stuff was just fun.

A 32-year-old virgin gusher – really? Since he wasn't running to city hall for a marriage license any time soon, Aaron knew he wasn't going to see Michelle again. He wasn't ready to take on the responsibility that came with taking Michelle's virginity. Buh bye, Michelle. Here's hoping she found her very own Captain Ahab as Aaron hoped for smooth sailing when he returned to americansingles.com.

Here Comes the Bride
Rene Wins the Online Dating Lottery

Rene was a perky, cute, fun 32-year-old hard working publicist who was one of the first of our group to venture into online dating. We all thought she was crazy at the time – online dating was still new and we didn't know anyone who had tried it. People were still answering personal ads and using chat rooms on AOL. Rene picked salon.com, a pop culture site with a personals section. After scrolling through numerous ads, some with pictures and some without, she came upon a profile that caught her eye. It was well written, funny and even though it didn't have a picture, she decided to contact him. No photo? We definitely thought she was crazy.

His name was Dayan, he was her same age and at the time, was also a publicist. We thought there was no way in hell he was straight. Within two days of exchanging emails, they started speaking on the phone. Their first phone call lasted five hours. Well, publicists do have the gift of gab, right? They decided to make their first date a week later and Rene still had no idea what he looked like, but she didn't care. Online dating placed so much emphasis on physical appearance, but that didn't matter to Rene as long as he was a good guy. Um, but what if he was 90 years old? Or height challenged? Or an ex-con who spoke eloquently? So many bad possibilities. How could she go out with someone without seeing a photo? Well, kids, back in the old days, like really old, like 1998, there was something called blind dating. It would go something like this – your mother's neighbor Joan had a nephew who lived in another town, but was coming to visit one Sunday and thought you and he would make a cute couple. So your mother would call, you would balk, and in the end, you would be at Joan's house that Sunday waiting for her nephew Eugene to show up for afternoon tea. Hey, what about people who get placed in arranged marriages, huh? They marry COMPLETE STRANGERS. So who were we to give Rene shit about going out with a man she's never seen? It was truly a blind date.

Dayan suggested having drinks at Maeve's, an unpretentious neighborhood sports bar that served Budweiser on tap. For Rene, Maeve's was a great choice because the place was only five minutes from her house. And guess what? It was five minutes from Dayan's house, too. Geographically desirable, check.

She described to Dayan what she would be wearing for the date and he did the same. Ok, reader, this sounds so ridiculous to us now. Sometimes, Stacey won't even date a guy who doesn't have at least three photos on his profile. A girl can't be too careful these days. When Rene got to the bar, they spotted each other right away and both were happy with what they saw. Physically attractive, check.

They settled into a booth, ordered some drinks and began to get to know one another and what they find out even made cynical Stacey and Robin take a beat. That past January, both were sent to the Park Hyatt in Toronto for a press junket and for four weeks, they stayed in rooms three doors down the hall from each other. Later that same month, they actually had sat at the same table with their respective clients at another industry event. And, the biggest coincidence of all is that they lived two blocks from each other and Rene would trip on the cracked sidewalk in front of Dayan's house every day on her morning run and then laugh at the big dog sitting in the window. Little did she know then that the dog named Trotski and the house with the cracked sidewalk would one day be hers.

A year later, Stacey and Robin were greeters at Rene and Dayan's wedding in Union Station. At the reception, the groom got up to toast his bride and here's what he said:

> "Rene and I clearly crossed each other's paths so many times, and never stopped long enough to notice. We now know that fate threw up its hands in defeat after trying to get us together in every other way and forced us on to the internet. Online dating is like trying to win the lottery, but this time, we both hit the jackpot."

So Stacey went to the bathroom to hang herself and Robin started mentally writing her new profile and asked the wedding photographer to take some extra photos of her next to the big flower arrangement.

For those of you doubters who thought Rene and Dayan would never last, two years later beautiful Dashiel was born and soon after, brother Beckett joined him. Mother, father and sons are very happy. Happy ending, check.

The Return of Brian
"No One en Casa"

Dear reader, when I last left off, I told Brian to go to hell. You remember him, right? The lying sack of crap with the "mysterious" life and job. After we parted ways, I rejoined singlesnet and came across a profile without a picture that sounded awfully familiar. The description was exactly Brian to a tee. I just knew it was him and he was about to do the same thing he did to me to God knows how many other women who were hoping to meet their next boyfriend online. For the good of all female online daters, Brian had to be stopped.

So I gathered my posse of friends and we batted around ideas of how to get to him. We debated if that profile was really his, we contemplated hiring a private investigator, we ran Google search after Google search on his name and company – and you wouldn't believe the stuff we found out. Side note – the internet is some scary shit! Just from our amateur Cagney & Lacey detective work, we found records of a Brian XXXX from Tujunga, California (which is where he lived) who was married two years earlier in Las Vegas to a woman from Tujunga, and they were still currently living in Tujunga. Things that make you go hmmm. Let me tell you something, I'd been living in Los Angeles almost ten years and I still didn't know where the fuck Tujunga was let alone how to pronounce it. While I had nothing invested in him, this infuriated me. He jerked me around, wasted my time and I wanted to get some sort of closure.

First Step, Road Trip!

I may not have been able to pronounce Tujunga, but I was going to find it, dammit. It all started one night over a few drinks – ok, a lot of drinks. It was me, friends Katie and Marci, and everyone's favorite gay, Steve (see previous chapters.) Somewhere between Cosmos and margaritas, we decided to pay a visit to Brian's house to meet the alleged wifey. While I had never been to his place (well, duh), I knew where he lived – the street and the house number. We piled into my car and I'd like to say we wore big sun hats, dark sunglasses and some mustaches, but the best we could come up with in my car was a doggie car seat and some Ralph's plastic grocery bags. Steve suggested poking eye holes in the bags, but suffocation and KKK comparisons seemed a bit too much. Instead, we put the visors down, put our collars up and did our best Sherlock Holmes impressions. Get the motor running, head out on the highway....

Before long, we arrived at our destination – 265 "Liar Lane." Well, I thought it was 265... As we turned the corner, 265 came into view. We got closer and ducked down in our seats (which is so lame because Brian never met any of my friends, so how would he know what they looked like), and slowly approached the house. That's when we all started hearing the mariachi music playing, noticed the 1985 Pontiac low-rider propped up on cinder blocks in the driveway and saw

32 Mexican children running amuck in what was clearly a run-down small apartment complex.

Steve: *Well, no wonder why he never invited you to his place. His Mexican wife would kill you muerto. Are these ALL of his kids?*
Stacey: *Idiot, this can't be his house.*
Marci: *The address does say 265, Stacey.*
Stacey: *But there's a piñata hanging from the railing. This clearly cannot be where he lives.*
Katie: *Um, what's wrong with piñatas?* (Oops, Katie is Mexican.)
Steve: *Hey, don't call me an idiot. You're the one who went out with the guy married to Selma Hayek.*
Marci: *Stace, your first date was at El Torito.*
Katie: *People, stop dissing my roots and let's think about this. What if it's not 265, but 562?*

Katie, the voice of reason. We continued driving up the street where the neighborhood slowly began to change. The further we went, the nicer the houses got which is not unusual for L.A. neighborhoods. By the time we hit Brian's block, it looked like suburbia with middle class homes complete with white picket fences and manicured lawns. If one of these was his house, I was going to fucking kill him. I could have so lived there.

As we approached 562, we could see the house was under renovation. New siding, new front porch and some tiling on the roof being worked on by a dozen... wait for it... Mexican workers. Maybe they lived at 265 "Liar Lane." Made their commute easy, right? But I digress.

We were hoping those workers could confirm if Brian was married or not. Steve decided he would be the one to go all Columbo on the situation, so he approached a worker.

Steve: *Hola, I'm looking for my friend Brian, he owns this house. Is he home?*
Worker: *No one en casa.*
Steve: *Is his wife around?*
Worker: *No one en casa.*
Steve: *Are the kids home?*
Worker: *No one en casa.*
Steve (on a hunch): *Would you like a ham and cheese sandwich?*
Worker: *No one en casa.*

Alrighty then. So Steve began snooping around, peering in windows and checking the mailbox, but to no avail. And when another worker pulled into the driveway, Steve wet himself and ran like a little girl screaming "no one en casa" back to the car. Mission aborted.

Second Step, Katie Joins Singlesnet

Well, since Operation Tujunga didn't go as planned, it was time to move to Plan B. I knew just how to get to Brian and so I created the perfect profile for Katie on singlesnet. Katie, in her early 30's, was a spitfire adorable Latina woman whom I knew Brian would like instantly. And I was right. It only took one flirt before Brian emailed her back with a long email. If there were any doubts it was him before, they were settled now. Not only did he send her his photo, he miraculously lost eight years because now he was telling Katie he was just 28 years old.

Come on, really, Brian? Once we confirmed Brian's interest, I took over Katie's emails. It was as if I turned into Elliot Ness and I was determined to bring Brian down. I began corresponding with Brian as Katie on a regular basis. Before long, he wanted to exchange phone numbers so I went to Best Buy and bought a go-phone for Katie to use. I sent Brian tantalizing texts to continue to pique his interest (which wasn't too difficult) and he would leave Katie ridiculously cheesy voicemails in return. A personal favorite was how he "longed to gaze lovingly into her eyes while they sipped his 85-year-old bottle of Glenfiddich and fed each other chocolate covered strawberries under the stars." Give me a fucking break – they never even spoke!

Okay. Two days later. Robin, Katie, Steve and I were driving to Vegas. I got us a free suite a new hotel, The Palazzo, with unlimited access to the concierge lounge (of which Steve and Robin took total advantage.) On the drive there, right before we hit the gigantic thermometer (that somehow Robin didn't see), the go-phone rang in the backseat. Shit, it was Brian! Awesome! This began a whole weekend of phone calls between Brian and Katie. He gave her the same lines and bullshit he gave me about his sick grandfather, his crazy work schedule, forgetting his cell phone in random places, etc. Ho hum, so unoriginal. If he only knew I was sitting next to her the entire time she was talking to him.

So, in the end, Vegas was a great trip. I got another comped weekend, Robin won $300, Steve got a blow job in the casino and Katie made a date with Brian only to chicken out when it counted. All we really needed her to ask Brian was if he had been to San Diego. One little question that would have answered everything. Oh well, mission aborted... again.

P.S. At least Robin saw the gigantic thermometer on the ride home.

Third Step, Brian Gets Down on One Knee

Dear reader, the following events are a true story. No matter how unbelievable it sounds, this shit really happened. No names were changed to protect the not-so-innocent. And even as I write this, it still sounds ridiculous, but in the end, you will give me props. Ready, here we go.

After the Katie fiasco and the 120 extra minutes I bought for that go-phone, we forgot about Brian. Honestly, we did. I started dating again and there were plenty of new guys for me to focus my attention on. Work was good, social life was good and Robin and I were well into writing this book. And four months later, my phone rings. Dum, da dum dum... guess who? Yep, Brian. I recognized the number immediately, but I didn't pick it up. In his message, he apologized for the way things were left between us, but I never called him back.

Two months later, I'm at work and my cell phone rings.

Stacey: *Hello?*
Brian: *Oh, hi sweetie, it's Brian.*
Stacey: *Brian who? Brian Austin Green from 90210? I loved you as David Silver.*
Brian: *Very funny. It's Brian XXXX.*
Stacey: *Oh, that Brian.*
Brian: *I totally deserved that. But please, hear me out and let me explain. I want to apologize to you for everything that happened. I never meant to hurt your feelings – it*

was just a case of me not being able to handle my life and everything that was going on at the time we were together.

Stacey: *So why didn't you just say that?*

Brian: *I didn't want to take a chance I'd lose you, but there was never anyone else. In fact, I've barely even dated anyone since you. I drive by your street all of the time and think about you. Please meet me for a drink and let me explain things.*

At this point, there were three things going through my mind – one, why does this guy keep popping back into my life? Two, I honestly was curious to hear what he had to say. And three, Robin and I did need to finish writing this book. So, I agreed to meet him for a drink, which ended up being at my apartment thanks to some L.A. traffic. Here's how it went down.

When he walked in the door, I was… ambivalent. Too much time had passed and too many lies told in between. But I'd be lying if I didn't say he still looked good. He awkwardly hugged me and sat down on the couch with a beer. Some small talk followed, he put down his beer, and launched into his diatribe of excuses and explanations for his behavior. And what happened next just floored me.

Brian: *Stacey, I know it's been a while, but there has never been another woman like you. Every date I go on only makes me think about you and how I screwed things up. You can't deny there was something special between us – we want the same things out of life and we'd be so great together. I want to be with you and I promise it will be different this time. Just give me the chance to get to know me. I'm begging you for another chance.*

And reader, he did just that. He begged me... on his hands and knees in my living room. He crawled, really, he crawled. No, seriously, crawled over to where I was sitting and literally pleaded for a second chance. Holy crap! No man had ever gotten on his hands and knees, much less crawled, for me. And in that moment, I actually thought about getting back with him. What the hell was he going to do next? Pull out that little Tiffany blue box we all want to see at some point? Wait a minute, was I being punk'd? Did they still even make Candid Camera?

Ok, decisions, decisions... While I was totally over him, I was impressed and touched by his display of emotions and humility. He took full responsibility for ruining the relationship the first time around and was promising he had changed. I asked myself if people could really change?

Fourth Step, the More Things Change, the More they Stay the Same

Well, reader, while I'd like to be able to report that Brian and I rode off into the sunset together and I'm living in that remodeled home in Tujunga, the reality is he was the same douchebag he always was. I guess I never really believed his theatrics that night, but I agreed to try to get to know him again to see if he had really changed. A few phone calls and a lot of promises, but in the end, Brian went right back to the same elusive behavior as the first time. The difference was that this time, I just didn't care. It was more like an experiment, but I wasn't invested. Brian's motives will always be a mystery to me, and it makes me wonder how many other men online do the same thing and why. Clearly, when it comes to Brian, there is "no one en casa."

Yabba, Dabba, Don't
What the Hell was Stacey Thinking?

I met Brad on plentyoffish the second day after I signed up. He was 34, gainfully employed as a crew member on a popular HBO comedy, and lived deep in the Valley – like where they shoot porn. Ok, not exactly geographically desirable and physically, not really my type at all. Think a younger, slimmer John Goodman. But he was funny on the phone, attentive and couldn't wait to meet me.

For our first date, he took me to Gladstone's on the beach in Malibu – not bad at all. We got along great, and he was fun to be around like a big kid. He was the kind of guy who talked to everyone at a party and if no one was having a good time, he'd put the lamp shade on his head. He was tall, had great hair, but to be honest, a little schlubby.

I didn't care though – I liked him and he liked me... a lot. Really liked me... a lot. He came on fast and furious. By the second date, he drunk dialed me from his friend's BBQ to tell me how much he liked me. On the third date, he told me he was and I quote "falling for me." Whoa! Slow down, bud.

Even my friends made fun of how strong he was coming on and how much he called... and called... and called. Brad instituted daily morning greetings the first week we started dating. He would wait for me to get up for work and ring! Every morning. Without fail. It was sweet, right? Ok, a little much, but I liked the attention.

Soon we were spending every weekend together and days in between. After a while, it became apparent that yes, Brad did really like me. Want to know what else he really liked? His friends Sam Adams, Stella Artois, Bud Weiser and Mr. Pabst Blue Ribbon. Beer for breakfast, beer for lunch and then some beer with his nachos at dinner. His favorite thing to do on a Sunday? Sit at the bar at the local Islands and drink, one guess... come on, bingo! Bottomless beer in a frosted glass. In fact, Islands was like a second home to this guy. The entire staff knew him by name and even gave him an employee t-shirt. I was so proud.

The first time I met his friends was at a bar (shocking) for a birthday party. They all loved me, but I was unnerved that this group of men, all in their mid-thirties and up, were drinking like John Belushi in Animal House. But I really wanted a boyfriend, so bring on the Bud. However, when Brad blew off our plans the next day to keep drinking his beer because he was so hung over from the night before, I stopped in my tracks and said we should stop seeing each other. And Brad freaked out.

He was so adamant about how much he liked me and needed to see me, that I overlooked it and the rest of the flags that were emerging – like he had no ambition, was totally lazy, had no ability to plan for things, and was honestly, an alcoholic. The more time I spent with him, the more he started to look like Fred Flintstone. Here was a guy with a pretty cool job and all he would do is wait for the bell to ring at the end of the day so he could go to the bar. In my head, he was Fred sitting on that dinosaur waiting for the baby pterodactyl to screech at 5pm. So why did I still like him? Yabba dabba do!

Well, he was a good guy who just needed some stability in his life, which I thought I was providing. So, as the relationship progressed, I felt it was time to introduce him to my core group of friends who gave him a huge thumbs up. Why wouldn't they? He was personable, fun-loving and really won Robin over when he artfully removed the broken cork from her wine bottle. This guy was in. After two and half months, he told me was getting ready to commit to me. Wow, a big step, unsolicited, and that was definitely exciting, but I had my reservations, which I could spell out in four letters – B-E-E-R.

Side note, while I was dating Brad, Robin and I were writing this book. Halfway through the process, we decided to stage a celebrity reading of some of the chapters. It turned into an exciting event in a theater filled with the most important people in our lives in attendance - friends, co-workers and industry contacts. I introduced Brad as my *friend* and went about my business getting ready for the show. Unbeknownst to me, Brad, with a perpetually full wine glass in hand, introduced himself to every single person in that fucking theater and told them we were a couple.

After a successful reading which went better than Robin and I could ever have imagined, we decided to take the cast and our friends out to a bar to celebrate. Brad, and the friend he brought with him – let's call him Barney - also came. While Robin and I stayed back at the theater to talk to people and wrap things up, Brad and Barney headed to the bar early and were there to meet the cast as they filed in. By the time I arrived a half hour later, I was met with shouts of congratulations from the entire cast and crew – they had just spent the last thirty minutes with Brad who made no qualms about telling everyone he was my boyfriend. **My boyfriend**. My committed, loving boyfriend. According to the cast, he picked up his Bud and declared his love for Stacey, dude.

The very next day Brad broke up with me. Take a beat and let that sink in. Got it? Broke up with me. Let's read it again, shall we? **He broke up with me**. 24 hours after telling almost every single person who mattered to me in life that he's my boyfriend.

Really? I mean, *really*? Yep. And this was his excuse – "I just can't do this. I really like you, Stacey. I just don't think ultimately you're the girl for me. I'm so sorry because I think you're a way awesome chick and I had the best time with you, but it's moving too fast and I am not a commitment guy." So why the hell did he and Barney go to our show and introduce himself to everyone as my boyfriend? Who does that? God, what would Wilma and Betty do?

That overweight, beer swilling frat boy who came on like gangbusters was dumping me. **HE WAS DUMPING ME?** I was the best fucking thing that had or ever would happen to him. Looking back, I don't even know why I was dating someone who drank too much and didn't have a single aspiration for the present or the future. Even though I knew I deserved better than Brad, I liked the guy. To this day it still puzzles me why he went to the reading and did what he did. He certainly didn't go there to network because he didn't have any ambition. Obviously, he wasn't there because he cared about me. Was it because of the open bar? Robin and I spent $500 on wine. Yeah, that was probably it.

Well, Brad, good luck meeting your next girl at the local dive bar. Maybe you'll be able to upgrade and end up with the waitress at the Islands where you spend so many of your Sunday afternoons... and Monday, and Tuesday, and Wednesday nights. Know what? I heard they're opening a new Applebees in the same strip mall as your Islands. You can mix it up on the weekends. Yabba, dabba, whatever, dude. Good riddance.

Elvis' Date Has Left the Building
Bella Meets a Hound Dog

Bella was a pretty 33-year-old with dark hair and eyes and an overall exotic appearance who was burned out on going to bars and clubs and dating Hollywood wannabes. For her first foray into online dating she chose salon.com, a site for the avant garde and artistic. After a quick perusal of the profiles, she spotted a guy who made her look twice, so she read his profile. BlueSuedeShoes57 was tall, dark and seemed to have a great sense of style – all of the things that were important to Bella. She always wanted to date a guy who was cooler than cool. Let's face it, she wanted to date an L.A. hipster who liked to "bust a moby" (dance), liked to drink "bronsons" (beer) and was looking for a "tassel" (girlfriend.) Who knew we'd need a Berlitz guide to write this story.

Bella emailed BlueSuedeShoes57 and he responded quickly. With that screen name, we'll give you one guess as to what his name was... no, it wasn't Sebastian, Lennon or Darian or whatever's hot with the hipsters today. It was... wait for it... Elvis. Yep, for reals.

Date #1 Fools Rush In

Their first date was something right out of the movie "Swingers." Elvis picked up Bella in a mint condition, sweet, black 1957 Cadillac complete with fins, whitewall tires and big dice hanging from the rear view mirror. He was wearing typical hipster fare – vintage clothing also known as "used." But to Bella, that was magical. He took her to Lotus, an Indian place in an artsy neighborhood, where they drank martinis (shaken, not stirred, of course), ate curried lamb and tandoori chicken (right out of the tandoori clay oven, of course), and smoked clove cigarettes (but, of course.) The date went so well, it continued on to The Dresden, an old school place in another artsy neighborhood where the aura of Vince Vaughn hovered over them. Elvis was a painter who often did showings at local galleries and in his spare time, participated in poetry readings. Bella was swooning and when he dropped her off for the night, the kiss was electric. She was all shook up.

Date #2 Love Me Tender

For their second date, Elvis invited Bella to his house for dinner because he wanted to cook for her. We're betting that's not all he wanted to do for her. Elvis lived in Echo Park and it doesn't get any more hipster than that. For those of you not familiar with L.A., think Williamsburg in New York. When she arrived at his apartment, she was floored. It was completely decorated like his car – super retro with a 1950's chrome and formica kitchen, a naugahyde cocktail bar, lava lamps and an actual select-o-matic jukebox complete with a full selection of 45's. Maybe Fonzie was his roommate. This place was absolutely "deck" (or cool, see Berlitz.)

So, reader, at this point in a date, we would want to know more about Elvis. Where was he from? What was his family like? Was his name really Elvis? But not Bella. All she cared about was how hot he looked and how cool he appeared. We know this sounds superficial, but it made her happy. While we were singing Suspicious Minds, Bella was humming Hunka Burning Love the next morning when she left his "pad."

Date #3 Heartbreak Hotel

For the third date, Elvis was upping his game when he invited Bella to go with him to the VH1 Music Awards. Supposedly he had a lot of connections in the music industry and one of them came through with VIP tickets to the event. Ok, readers, even we were impressed by this date. Bella was super excited as we hit Melrose Ave. to find her the perfect outfit for the night. After all, VIP meant hanging with celebrities, parties and the red carpet! This was going to be an amazing night and we found ourselves a little jealous of Bella's new found King.

On the night of the big event, Bella had her hair and make-up done at the salon and spent several hours getting ready. She eagerly awaited Elvis' arrival and when she heard the familiar honk of his Caddy, she hurried downstairs. When she walked outside, imagine her surprise when she found Elvis leaning against his car, wearing a white polyester, sequined jumpsuit with butterfly collar, blue suede platform shoes, hair in a pompadour and gold sunglasses to boot. Holy crap, he looked like a fucking Elvis impersonator from the Vegas strip. She was mortified. How could she be seen in public with this guy especially at such a high profile event? Oh, don't be cruel, Elvis. You've just shattered Bella's dream because her once cool hipster was actually just a freak.

Lawdy, lawdy Miss Clawdy, Bella was caught in a trap and didn't know how to get out. Elvis jumped in the car and she went with him. God bless her. When they arrived at L.A.'s prestigious Shrine Auditorium, they made their way down the red carpet and all Bella could hear were the photographers shouting: "Elvis, smile" and "Elvis, is that your new Priscilla?" When one reporter asked him if he was part of the show, Elvis's face lit up like neon sign. This guy was in his glory and Bella couldn't get inside fast enough.

Finally indoors, Elvis handed the tickets to the usher and Bella was relieved they'd soon be sitting. Lady Gaga was bound to be dressed worse than Elvis – maybe people wouldn't even notice him. Who was she kidding? The way he looked, even Stevie Wonder would notice him. As they started to walk down the aisle towards the orchestra section, the usher quickly corrected them by pointing to the stairs where they proceeded to climb all the way to the second to last row in the highest balcony (also known as the nose bleed seats.) VIP, my ass.

All of a sudden, chill Elvis turned into the psycho Elvis who shot up his television. He went ape shit on this poor usher throwing him up against the wall and demanding he re-seat them downstairs. The usher was at a loss and Bella couldn't believe what she was seeing. Any effort to calm him down was fruitless as he pushed her aside and stormed to the box office. Not knowing what else to do, Bella followed him. Once at the Will Call window, he screamed at the agent to give him his VIP tickets and she politely informed him there weren't any such seats left for him.

Bella was shocked as she watched the veins in his neck start to bulge and his eyes bug out of his head. He was practically foaming at the mouth like a rabid hound dog.

Elvis (screaming at the top of his lungs): *"Don't you know who I am?"*
Will Call Lady (calmly): *"Yes, Sir, you're the hired Elvis impersonator for the red carpet. I'm sorry, there are no other seats available to you."*

Say what? He's the what?? Here Bella was thinking he was Michaelangelo, Da Vinci, Allen Ginsberg and Jack Kerouac all rolled into one. But he paints and writes poetry, right? Doesn't he? Bella grasped at mental straws, but it was no use. This guy was nothing but an Elvis impersonator who actually believed he was Elvis. And he was kinda violent to top it off. Great, he wasn't even cool Elvis – he was the pill popping, died on his toilet Elvis. Jesus Christ.

While Elvis was still causing a ruckus and security approached, Bella slipped out of the building and into a cab before she became part of a scene in Jailhouse Rock. The next day he sent her flowers to apologize and she refused them. Return to sender, address unknown.

Happily Ever After?
What Happened to Robin and Stacey?

So readers, we're sure you're wondering whatever happened with our quest for love. Well, this book was two years in the making and a lot has changed for the both of us since we started writing. 2010 was a "banner" year as we were both laid off from our uber-glamorous jobs that we dutifully served for ten years each. Employment, re-location, finding love or still looking – wait til you hear this!

Stacey

When I last left you, I had just been dumped by Fred Flintstone and frankly, I was ready to throw in the towel on the online dating craze. Just as I signed on to singlesnet to hit "cancel," I got an email from a guy who didn't have his photo posted. Normally that would be a deal breaker, but honestly, I had no plans on dating again, so it didn't matter at the time. His email was funny and polite so I responded, but without any intentions of following through. At that point, I had my job, I had my dog, we just did a successful reading of the first part of this book, and the season finale of "The Real Housewives of New Jersey" was coming on – what more could I ask for in life?

But "No Photo Jason" kept emailing and before I realized it, a couple of weeks had gone by and I had kinda started an online "thing" with this guy. He was really funny and very bright, but I didn't have any plans to meet him, so I had no idea who I was chatting with – he could have been Chaz Bono for all I knew. Then one day he said: "How can I ask you out if you don't know what I look like? Don't you want to see my picture?" Since I was a new and independent woman who had resolved herself to dying alone, I told him to send the photo, but truthfully, no expectations. When the picture arrived, I was speechless. The online dating Gods had thrown me a curve ball. Just when I thought I was out, they pulled me back in because "No Photo Jason" was gorgeous. Now, let's be clear – Jacques880 hadn't started working for singlesnet since he had his lucrative career at match.com, my membership wasn't nearly expired and I was pretty sure it wasn't Brian using someone else's photo. Jason seemed to be the real deal. He was in his early 30's, from the South and full of charm, tall and really fucking handsome. Even though we never discussed our jobs, there was no way I wasn't going to meet this guy now. I know, readers, we just told you a dozen stories about guys who didn't look anything like their picture. But there was something different about Jason – I couldn't describe it, I just knew.

For our first date, he suggested a really nice restaurant called Café des Artistes– one of **the** best French restaurants in the city. How did he know how much I loved French food? As the date got closer, I actually found myself getting nervous.

Dammit! This is exactly what I didn't want to happen. When I walked into the Café, he was seated in the back – definitely tall, dressed in a sports coat and button down shirt and looked even better than his photo. Seriously, I swear. He took my breath away. Before I sat down, he stood up and I would have to admit his good manners threw me off my game. He had already ordered wine and cheese. Wine and cheese, people! This guy had class! What was supposed to be just drinks and appetizers soon turned into a three hour dinner and dessert date. The conversation was effortless and he told me the reason he picked this restaurant was because he was completely enamored with Paris after taking his first trip the year before. Wait, I also took my first trip the year before and was also crazy about Paris. We soon realized we were there at the same time. We probably were in line for the Louvre standing next to each other. This was too good to be true – I felt a connection to this guy. So obviously, there had to be something wrong with him, right? Everything seemed perfect, but he was very cagey about what he did for a living. Here I was feeling bowled over by him and he was probably a bank robber, porn star or the guy who flipped real estate signs on Ventura Blvd. Figures.

Robin

Yes, it's true. After ten years of hard work, dedication and countless hours, I was laid off. And you know what? I was happy about it because I was burnt out. Seriously, this was the first time in my entire adult life that I didn't have to go to work. I finally had time to reflect on my life. So, what did I want out of it? To get married – well, you already know that. To write books – ok, you're reading one now. To be happy – I was still having trouble with that one. When I was offered a job at Warner Bros. and turned it down, I knew in my heart it was time for a change. So I packed up my car and headed straight for... wait for it... Florida! Now you're asking why Florida? I couldn't afford to live in L.A. on unemployment and I had already tried dating every available dude in his 40's in the area; I wanted to be back on the east coast but New York was way too cold; and I had family in Florida which meant free rent for a while. Boo-yah!

Despite popular belief, South Florida isn't filled with just grandparents, retirees and people who go there to die. Florida was a grab bag of opportunity for me. There were many cities, including my new home of Ft. Lauderdale, where young professional social lives were alive and kicking. There were plenty of people without pacemakers, dentures and oxygen tanks. In fact, the Hard Rock casino was just steps from my front door. There were a lot of options. If I wanted to hang with rich Polo players, I could head to Wellington; if I wanted to meet a rocker I could go to Vince Neil's bar "Dr. Feelgoods" in West Palm Beach; and if I was feeling the old folks, I could always visit my mother in her retirement community where my own Thurston Howell III was waiting for me.

While I was getting used to my new surroundings and meeting people, you know I had to check out the online dating scene in Florida so I went with plentyoffish.com because unemployment wouldn't cover match.com's high fees. Fasten your seat belts because here we go again!

Stacey

Six months later, Jason and I were still dating. He finally confessed to what he did for a living – aside from his tech day job, he was an actor and writer. But like for real, not a Hollywood cliché. He actually had an acting resume and things he had written. And they were good. Not like the rest of this town who say they "write" or "act" but follow it up with "would you like the Caesar or house salad?" The reason he didn't tell me what he did right away was because he didn't want me to think he was dating me for my career and the possibility I could help him. This was truly too good to be true. So what could I say, life was going great. Robin and the rest of my friends loved Jason, the dog was healthy, my job was thriving, and Jason and I soon took the relationship to the next level. We were now a real couple. Pulled down the profiles and declared it on Facebook kind of couple. Cause you know if you put it on Facebook, it's gotta be real. We took our first weekend trip together and all was right in the world.

And then... I was fired. Ok, fine, laid off but it still felt like being FIRED! Working on the number one comedy on television and being told my contract wasn't going to be renewed is still a nice way of saying I was FIRED. During the worst recession this country has seen since The Great Depression. And unlike happy-go-lucky Robin who was leaving to go to Florida, I wasn't fucking happy about it. I was scared and sad. It sucked.

So, let's review, shall we? First Robin got laid off (fired) and I was about to lose one of my closest friends and writing partner to Florida. Then I got laid off (well, fired.) And in the natural progression of how my life works, Jason also got laid off (yep, fired.) During this trying time which would have broken up most couples actually only made us stronger. We moved in together, collected unemployment together and claimed free crap off Coke bottle caps together. But most importantly, I found my soulmate. He's loving, kind, talented, smart, funny, and I could go on. Jason's the one, for real.

(P.S. We'll work for food.)

Robin

Unlike L.A., the responses I'd gotten to my profile on plentyoffish have been overwhelming. Many, many dates with men between 45 and 55 years old. However, what I've noticed about the guys in Florida is this – it's shocking how many men do not know how to have an introductory conversation with a woman without spilling all of the ugly details in the first thirty seconds. These are men who managed to get married and have children at some point in life. Let's take John, for example. John was a 48-year-old owner of a landscaping company who lived in West Palm Beach and was divorced with two children. This was our first phone conversation verbatim:

Robin: *Hi, John, it's Robin from plentyoffish returning your call.*
John: *Hey, how you doing?*
Robin: *Good, how about yourself?*
John: *Doing good, can't wait to get back to work.*
Robin: *Were you on vacation?*

And here we go.

John: *No. I was diagnosed with colon cancer three months ago. They cut out ten centimeters of my colon and yesterday I was declared cancer free. So, I'm really happy about that considering a year ago, I broke both of my feet which was my own fault. Cause you know I have two daughters and I didn't want to worry them because my oldest daughter, who lives with me, her mother died from cancer. And my youngest daughter, who's being raised by my relatives in Ohio, well, her mom is just gone.*

Robin (first chance to say anything): *Gone? Where did she go?*

John: *Let's just say she's just gone. And then to top it off, while I was drinking in a bar last night, someone keyed my car and I know who did it. And I'm going to find him.*

Robin: *Uh, John, that's my other line ringing and I really need to take this call. I'll call you back....*

Yeah, I'll call him back, um, NEVER! See what I mean? Who would say all of that in a first phone call? You'd be surprised how many I've had like that.

Yes, I miss L.A., my friends and the canyons, but I'm enjoying my new home and I look forward to what life has to offer me in Florida as well as a new collection of online dating stories. So, get ready, reader, volume two will be coming soon. But most of all, I'm looking forward to getting my happy ending like Stacey.

(P.S. Will work for food.)

Addendum

These are Actual Emails

Be Afraid. Be Very Afraid.

A Country in Crisis
Illiteracy is Rampant in America

As we wrote this, President Obama was trying to fix America's healthcare issues, the rising gas prices and end the Iraqi war. But, why, oh why, has he not addressed the real crisis facing this country everyday? A crisis of epidemic proportion. A crisis so frightening, that if it's not taken care of, can threaten the balance and sanctity of our entire nation! For the love of God, IS EVERYONE ILLITERATE?

Dear reader, please look at some of the emails we received for yourselves and you be the judge. We say it's time for a nationwide crackdown for the good of every American citizen. Note these are verbatim – God help us all.

1) **jjsexnow, 28 years old from La Habra, CA**
   ya im cute.i can send you my picture.just give me cell number so i can send you a taxes pic or call me at 714 XXX-XXXX so we can chat live you hot cake.so hit me back with yo cell number. ps im jason m.

**Hi Jason, thanks for the offer, but I already have someone who does my taxes.*

Best, Hotcake

2) **christopher28, 30 years old from Simi Valley, CA**
hey sweety u look very sexy and pretty and nices and everything that i think that i would like about u and i like to know can i call u and talk to u and are u at home and would u like to meet me and would u like to come here to my house to see me and to be with and to know me be person and by phone

**No you can't call me and no I'm not home and no I won't come to your house and I'm not really that nices.*

3) **mikky020, 47 years old from Aberdeen, MD**
Hello,
How are you doing today? I am michael by name,i search my other half from which I can build reliable and strong relationship in life,one who will take me there where i have always dreamnt....well i am single and looking for the right woman to hold the keys to the door of my heart,you seem to be a wonderful woman.All my life i have always nursed the dream of being with a woman who's loving,caring and honest a woman that keeps to her words one who is very surportive of her other half any day any time,someone i can trust,a woman that will be there for me for good or bad.I know what it will lead me to loving and caring for you,when i fall deeply in love,it's to the extent that i can't control my feelings anymore and getting hurt at the end but i am sure you

are not that type of a woman that plays GAMES with peoples heart. I know that every day our hearts would be each others and our feelings become more passionate and strong forever till the edge of time....Your heart would be fixed by me,all depends if you give me the chance to show you how much I care for you.I know that somewhere in our big world out there,there you are to love me,care for me and preserve me..I wouldlove to be the man that will take your breath away,chase away the loneliness in you and make you happy for the rest of your life..I search for reliable support in the woman of my dream,the woman who will love me and respect my feelings for her it is for me the main thing,the other half I understand may be older than me or just perfect match for me,but I think that it's a big plus for us.I want to make a right choice cos i have been faced with stuffs and i wont want to go there anymore.I very much hope that I am of interest to you and believe things will work out the way i wished to give to you.Also that we could become friends and if fate wants we become more than friend and make the magic work for just more than one night i need a woman who is truthful to her words and also trustworthy.Here is my personal Email where you could email me cos i hardly come on here mic_phil1@ yahoo.com you can email me on there for better hook-up ok or better still if you have Yahoo messenger my ID is XXXX buzz me up sometime if you care.Hope to hear from you real soon and do take good care of yourself for me till i hear from you.I care and i believe you are that Woman i so much desire to rule my world.HUGS AND KISSES

********MIchael*********

**Hi, Michael. We don't know each other. In fact, this is the first email I've even gotten from you. How can you know my heart needs to be fixed by you? Good luck with all of your stuffs.*

4) pachik, 43 years old from Los Angeles, CA

hi my rill name is Armenak i am poet i like your photo i dont know your personality but i hope youare good greal , my pomes abut life comunication for exempl , you are my imagination ,let criait somting now for love comunication for happynes for now game i vont tostart am here agan. thenk you my cell is 323 XXX-XXXX

Dear Armenak, I am good and greal. I wish much happynes and best of luck criaiting somting.

5) ieshadow88, 43 years old from Los Angeles, CA

this ieshadow88 so whats girl i would send pic but its easyer to just meet some places dont you think well sends i have no pictures of my self i well tellyou what i look like 6;1 inchs tall about two hundred pounds blue eyes brown hair ahole lot of tatoos 43 years old and really would like to meet you ieshadow88 hope to here from you soon late

Dear ieshadow88, since you're only 6 inches tall, I'm afraid it won't work. Good luck, ahole.

6) williamrh, 39 years old from Glendora, CA

hahaah the africans i have ran into many hahahaah all they want is money hahahaa i just see the africa crap i just delete hahaah well im william im ready to get started marrie a awsome woman have really great hot sex and have babys live life good bbqs family and love love love and thats the truth im not bashfull at all i dont lie sell out and take any bs from any one i really want a good woman ill love her and everything abbout her im 39 and happy healthy and alone hehe but hoptfully not for long. im a bullfrog that you can make into a king i know how to , i know things abbout woman that will make me a sucessfull husband and partner. if your not impressed then tell me we dont fit hahaha rejection is not bad. getting to know someone and finding out something that is not acceptable and having to end it is bad. ihave a painless plan for the selection process really and you will learn abbout your self to. im william take care byby

Dear williamrh, good luck having hot sex and babys. Hahahahah.

7) **lifetrack, 42 years old from Columbus, OH**

Hello,

How are you doing hope everything is great i am Richard XXXX i am 40 yrs old from GA and i have blue eye balls with black hair i am 6 fit tall an average body shape with a sexy lips and eyes. I have been divorced for 4 yrs now living alone feeling lonely with my dog at home no one to take care of my things during my business period so therefor i can believe the capture of my eyez and heart on you the moment i set my eyez at your pic it was so amazing to find someone so sweet on earth again and for that i would like to know more about you cos i found you as my perfect match and as my soul mate in the result of your profile and i would like you to be the only one for me i am honest caring and understanding person and i am a good seducer i can treat on a better treat you like a queen love you for who you are and i wouldn't like you to be worried about the distances between us cos distance has nothing to do with relationship and love, so i would like you to send me your yahoo ID so we can chat better there or if you can Im Me Or Add me To Your List xxx@yahoo.com so we make conversation on love i need you so much in my life.

Thanks

Dear lifetrack, I'm afraid I'm not a woman who will take care of your things during your business period. And blue eyes balls freak me out.

8) ericstls, 30 years old from Covina, CA

iam look for a tiking good heart worimg women that nise . that dust on chet iam going to love that women all my heart

Dear ericstls, ??

9) cowboydance, 52 years old from Bakersfield, CA

hmm if our eyes met while in an isle at the grocery store.. you would definatly get a wink from me.. Then when you followed me to the meat counter and asked me how to pick out the perfect steak.. I would show you what to look for and maybe ofer to bbq it for you.. haha you are sooo cute.. come here.. :)

Dear cowboydance, I love to vacation on the Isle of Grocery Store! Right up there with Jamaica and Belize, but my favorite is the Isle of Produce – it's so green!

10) e.matt, 29 years old from Arvada, CO

Hello cutie,
How you doin' there? Hope you cool! Just registered to the website homie and been though your profile but hey, can't keep out'a here without saying hello. I care to know more about you, what you think 'bout that? Matthew XXXX is the name and camping, biking, and lot more is the game which you could know after a response to this message. I'm also called Matt and i like it that way. I'm 33 with one kid. What'ya your real name and where you at? Have some pictures, don't know if you might like to see. Waiting to read from you. You can just send me a mail to my private email id xxxx@yahoo.com. Please, get back to me as soon as possible. Keep lookin good, preety face.
Holla back!

Matt.

Dear Matt, Yo, yo, yo homie. Holla.

Let's Talk About Sex, Baby Bow, Chika, Bow, Bow

To hell with an introduction, let's just have sex. Yep, that's it. That's all they've got to say. Oh, but of course, just let us know where and when. Fr-eaks!

1) **goofy1111arent, 41 years ago from Ripon, CA**
   hi. i know this sounds like a weird ? but what is your favorite position during sex? dont be affended just curios.

   joe

   Dear Joe, like I'd tell you.

2) **peaceman82, 35 years old from Los Angeles, CA**
   hi, your photo is charming and i guess you are really passionate.i can't wait to call you my betterhalf.you can make it with me because , i can feel you in my arms. love you babe.take good care of yourself for me.

   Dear peaceman82, not in this lifetime.

3) **bobbyluvu2, 40 years old from Hawthorne, CA**
can we make good passionate, and sweet love boo... smile.. just keeping it real... you know you wouldn't take me to see your parents.. but i bt you that if you go blk, you won't go back...lol

Dear bobbyluvu2, I'd die alone first. Boo.

4) **bobbyluvu2 again**
hello can i do some freakie shit to you, only for one niye.. then if we fine ourselves liking each other like that,, then we can hit it off like that.. ok.. what you say boo.. my name is bobby luv.. wat is yours..

Bobbyluvu2, feel free to practice that freakie shit by yourself.

5) **jamieyn, 43 years old from Stone Mountain, GA**
I'm James XXXX I cant wait to be your lover, I have read your profile and i must tell you that you sound so interesting and you are my ideal woman. I am caring, honest, romantic, loving, passionate,affectionate woman seeking for a caring, honest, passionate, romantic, sexual, faithful woman for a relationship that will lead to something really nice like .... mmmmmmm. Age,distance is irrelevant to me,i look at the mind.Write me or add through my id xxxx@ yahoo.com, If you are interested after viewing my profile and then i will tell you all about me,send pic's too.I am ready to play my role as you want me to , we study ourselves know how compatible we are and chemistry between us. Kissssssssssssss.
Take Care

Dear James, really, I can so wait for you to be my lover.

6) abk1588, 38 years old from Frazier Park, CA

hello my name is tony im38 im a single man i wouldk like to meet you read my profile abk1588 iam very cut guy and vey nice iwould love settle down with you babe i would go to bed with you and make a family togther iam alot of fun ineed a women in my life ilove the beach moves dinning out makeout im5'5 drak brown hair blue eyes medium bluit i have respect for women i wish we could meet eachother . ilove for you to come to frazierpark ca www.mapquest.com xxxx harriet rd, frazierpark ca 93225

give me a call great looking mmmmmmmmmm

Dear Tony, yes, what the world needs is for you to spread you seed. Keep mapquesting.

Heaven Sent
Who Knew Stacey and Robin Came Straight From Angels

Love, exciting and new. Come aboard, we're expecting you.

1) **jimmyparker03, 41 years old from Visalia, CA**
   Hello
   Hi Gorgeous one. How are you doing today ? hope you receive this message and it finds you well. My name is JIMMY XXXXX and I am contacting you from west africa .. were i am now for a buisness road contract awarded to me and i am originaly from VISALIA CA. I am a contractor, well i lost my wife some year ago so she is late and i have 1 son who i love so much is all i have now well i am 40 yrs and searching for an honest, mature, good lady who can treat me with dignity and respect. searching for a true love someone i can cater for and love as well but thought I'd take a risk! I'm looking for my other half the one who wants to out do each other in kindness and love each other unconditionally. Romance and handholding, candles

and kisses, respect and support are the things look for and the things I'd like to give. When I saw your profile I decided to respond with the hope of corresponding. I guess the first thing that came into my mind when I saw your photo was "WOW!!!". You are DROP-DEAD GORGEOUS!!! . It seems you are that rare woman who has just as much (or more) going for herself on the inside as the outside. I would consider it an honor to get to know you. I'm EXTREMELY busy so I'm not looking to move too fast or for anything serious at this point, but if sparks fly then so be it . About me, I don't have much time for or interest in the "traditional singles scene" so I decided to give this a try. Besides, I have a few friends who have had good time in the scene of internet dating so i decided to give it a trial. I find that many women I encounter don't call lately, my business has kept me from getting out much, but in general I don't have a problem meeting women. However, meeting the right woman has been somewhat challenging. I guess I'm seeking the proverbial "entire package"-beauty, brains, pleasant disposition, morals, compassionate heart and ethics. You certainly appear to fit that mold. Nothing speaks my interest more than a woman who has a great deal going for himself, yet carries herself as if she is oblivious to that fact. First and foremost I'm looking for a woman with the potential and desire to become my "best friend" because I believe that is the foundation for a lasting relationship. I'm sorry for the lengthy note, but my hope is to give you an accurate snapshot of who I am, especially since I dont have much about me in my profile. I don't know what else to tell you, but consider this: To laugh is to risk appearing a fool. To weep is to risk appearing sentimental. To reach out for another is to risk involvement. To expose feelings is to risk exposing of yourself. To play your ideas, your dreams, before the crowd, is to risk your loses. To love is to risk not being loved in return. To live is to risk dying. To hope is to risk despair. To try is to risk failure. But risk must be taken because the greatest hazard in life is risking nothing. And people who risk nothing, do nothing, have nothing, buy nothing. You may avoid suffering and sorrow, but you simply cannot learn, feel, cha Till i hear from you again, have a nice time.

some poems for u and i will write more for u okay

I can't promise you
that dark clouds
will never hover
over our lives
or that the future
will bring us many rainbows.
I can't promise you
that tomorrow
will be perfect
or that life will be easy.
I can promise you
my everlasting devotion,
my loyalty,
my respect,
and my unconditional
love for a lifetime.
I can promise that

I'll always
be there for you,
to listen
and to hold your hand,
and I'll always do
my best to make you happy,
and make you feel loved.
I can promise that
I'll see you through
any crisis,
and hope with you,
dream with you,
build with you,
and always cheer you on
and encourage you.
I can promise that
I'll share my dreams

You can send me an email to xxxx@yahoo. Com and if you care to chat you can add me to your list okay, I want you to know that i will be moving to your state after my project soon . Hope to hear from you soon. Thank you

Dear Jimmy, roses are red, violets are blue. Can't believe I'm wasting time emailing you. P.S. You say you lost your wife and she's late. Late? You mean left you?

2) sweetcurtis, 50 years old from Los Angeles, CA
Hello ..how are you?? My name is Curtis XXXX ,I just register into this dating site some days back after my horrible past years. I have been married twice. I lost

my first wife and one kid in a ghastly motor accident and i divorced my second wife when I caught her in bed with my Best friend .I have been heart broken ever since, and i have had trust issues which made me stay away from everyone including my friends for the passed 6years. But i know now is the time to come outta the shell and start a new life , i am done with the trust thing and wants to start life all over again, i am willing and ready to trust 100% with my heart i need a very decent, faithful and mature woman to trust my heart with, someone that will Trust and love me as much as i love and trust her.I am not after physical beauty but am after the beauty of the heart. I was impressed when I search and got to your profile, you look so cute, mature, responsible in appearance and above all my heart has never remained the same vere since i read and saw your pics and profile i have been looking at it for over 1hrs now.. just to make sure its not Lust and now i know it isnt . i just want to know u so much more just to confirm what my heart tells me and make u feel how i feel also my Heart tells me that you are my better half (I Listen to my heart and not to the Voice in my head).

Even though we are distance apart but I can easily fly to meet you wherever you are.

I dont believe that distance and age can be a barrier to having a smooth and good relationship.

I am a young gentle Man of 50 years old, from dublin ireland .But Lived In decatur Los angeles California in

The USA for about 9months .I am a major importer of Crude Oil and Gas, i am a boss of my own, i am an oil merchant. I am faithful in love, am caring. I can't promise you that in the future there will be no ups and downs or dark clouds in our lives or that the future will bring us a 100% satisfaction, But i can assure you that as long as i shall live and walk the face Of the earth U will have my heart, my trust, my love, and every Other thing that goes along with a good relationship that is filled with Love and 90% satisfaction, and my unconditional and pure love for more than a lifetime even Unto enternity and only a good woman deserves that, Just add me On my yahoo messenger ID xxxx@yahoo.com I will be very glad to hear from you, i am all i say i am, just add me on yahoo messenger and i will proove this to you. Please If You read this message Just let me know that you got it and at least Please Let me know if u are willing to talk to me by adding me on your Yahoo messenger or just send me your email address and i will add you.. I just want you to know that whatever i sent you on here is from my heart.. i dont tell everyone so much about me.. I will never do that.

Dear Curtis, step away from my profile.

3) **bengor3230, 37 years old from Los Angeles, CA**
hello am benard,
how you doing today.
My relationship with you i belive will to an end to a long time of lonelyness to this very day my heart still yurns for a very good friend that might grow into

something i realy want in life like a wild fire it just burns i have come to realize i gotta look beyond the sky if its meant to be he will come to me. The more i see, is the more i realize. i have found the power of love i never thought this true but i pray it work .Life is so unpredictable. Changes always come along, in big or small ways. I don't know what happened that this sudden change has turned my world upside down. I don't know exactly what it is, it just hit me, but there is something really special about you. Inside of me there is a place where my sweetest dreams reside, where my highest hopes are kept alive, where my deepest feelings are felt and where my favorite memories are safe and warm. I just hope some day you can the there too.

Dear Benard, my heart yurns for a guy who can speak English properly.

4) ramminit71, 36 years old from Los Angeles, CA

Hello, I'm Greg, i came accross your profile while searching on this site, and saw you so attractive and decided to email you. You are so pretty that i believe God spent extra time creating you and if i were to present your picture in heaven, all the angels would hide their faces in shame. I'm a gentle hearted man, i like making friends because friends are the best. Love is all about what is in the heart. what i care about is u are beautiful and i wish to be the man you've always wanted and i'm sure you and i would work things nicely beaing together. I like holding hands walking together side by side and sharing love vows and i see you as a woman i would love to do that with and cuddle with. like playing volleyball and also basketball. At my leisure hrs, i like going to the gym and also like going to watch movies. I've learnt to respect beauty very well thats why i respect you. I know that love has no distance, because what is meant to be will always find a way to be. So all that matters is for the two hearts to be together somewhere I've been divorced for many years now and i wish to settle down now t find a real Love. I have a Daugther and i'm proud to be her father. I work with a construction company in us and wish to relocate to find my missing rib. Can you please reply me at my private email so we could get to chat and make this conversation serrious and see where it takes us to. Hope to hear from you soon.

Dear Greg, good luck finding your missing rib. Sounds medically unsound.

5) omolebear, 45 years old from Los Angeles, CA

Hello,

how are you doing, i hope you are healthy today, cause your look and smile gives me the feeling that you are great, by the way my name is christian tracy, that which my parents christianed me, but my friends call me christ most of the times, am a student currently having my masters in architecture in the university, and i would be graduating soon, am very single and taking my time, to seek my mate, and the most important part, is following the lords lead, a friend of mine signed up this site for me, about two weeks ago, and he told me it was a nice site to find my mate, so, about two days ago, the lord revealed to me, to come search the site for my missing rib, that was why i came on here, and i got to search, and while searching, i saw your profile, it took my breath away immediately, your profile was great and genuine, i didnt know women of your kind still exist, you made me feel love is genuine, and at first sight, it might sound silly, but its the truth, i couldnt help but smile at every word you write, and say to my self, this is my missing rib, and i want to take this chance to get to know you better, a little about me , which i would want you to know, I dont play games, am very honest and truthful, you may be surprised, for if anything I am very honest even if it hurts to say it. I am trying this as a new step in my life...that is probably why it is so long...To me your feelings, thoughts and what you believe is the window into your heart, that is where true love and passion grows from, your looks would be a wonderful blessing, but the beauty inside is what makes the outside truly shine,I love the Lord Jesus the most, he is my reason for being, I am a gentleman by nature, and I mean not just opening car doors, the whole package. I am faithful, caring, loving and a passionate man. I feel that it is important to be friends and to communicate both directions for extended periods of time, to learn about each other and let that build trust and closeness. I believe in total honesty as well, and yes, even if it hurts, i love watching movies, i like going to the beach, the cinemas, i like eating, my favourite dish is spagetti, i like it because its easy to make, and one other thing, i like dancing, ballroom dance is my favourite, do you like to dance, would love to dance with you if you love to. i really would love to get to know you better, PLEASE EMAIL

ME DIRECTLY TO MY EMAIL ADDRESS, SO I CAN HAVE YOUR EMAIL PRIVATELY THERE ALRIGHT, BECAUSE I CHECK THAT EMAIL ALL THE TIME, its xxxx@yahoo.com, PLEASE CAN YOU DOWNLOAD YAHOOMESSANGER SO WE CAN CHAT, I HAVE JUST DOWNLOADED IT, my addy is christ_trustXX, add me there if you already have one, but if you dont, please download one to your computer so we can chat better, i would be honoured. please make sure you email me directly to my email address alright, so i can read your reply, cause i always check my emails there. please ensure you email me to my email address which is xxxx@yahoo.com. you get it, there is an _ between letters ok i await to hear from you alright.

thanks. from Christian

Dear Christian, your friends call you Christ??? I had no idea the son of God was emailing me.

6) Toslukas, 46 years old from New York, NY

Dear Angel
How Are you doing ,Just have just finished going through your profile, when my heart stop beating ,that's because Your smile has a beauty that I find in no other profile... As long as my heart beats, I shall seek out your soul and be fulfilled......!Every night I dream of heaven, and I'd gotten used to the idea that they are looking for an angel {YOU}, one that went missing the day you stepped into The word, the day men sorrows were washed away and men took a step into the impossible, crossing the margin from natural to

supernatural. You are an angel and forever you will be. The one whose memories men will treasure forever till the day thay turn into an angel like you. And i feel we are compactable......I wonder how God could let you go off so easily, you are an angel from heaven seeing you has made me believe that an angel is missing from heaven, And you're a Pretty Godess, WOW i never knew that one day i would be previledged to meet a woma like you in the universe, really i am impressed with your charming and irresistable looks, you have swept me off my feet sweetheart, quite enchanting and very captivating too. Am online now lest have a chat on yahoo IM xxxx@yahoo.com

from Jackson

Dear Jackson, sorry, but not many people are actually compactable with a true angel like myself.

7) **Tonykk2, 35 years old from Villa Park, IL**
My Name is Tony i am interested in you when i saw your profile you are such a tender, captivating, good looking lady have ever set my eyes on..... I will like to know you better if you wouldn't mind, what you do for leaving, marital status ,age location... and also i must confessed the Good work of God that i see in you, cause if i dont, it will be an issue boarding my mind..... I want you to know that God created you as a gifted soul and i want you to continue maintaining that cause if you dont,i wouldn't have meet such a pretty damsel like you, i must tell you the truth, i love your profile so much, and i want you to know that love is

not about finding the right person, but creating a right relationship. It's not about how much love you have in the beginning but how much love you build till the end and if it is meant to be, our hearts will find each other when we meet. And if our hearts melt together so will our bodies and souls. Then every word and every touch will fuel our passion flame, i will be looking forward to hearing from you soon, because i cant wait to read your reply. If you care to chat, i will like to have your yahoo im so that i can add you to my list and we can talk better and know more about each other, here is my yahoo IM (xxx@yahoo. com) add me to your list and let's chat, hope to hear from you soon asap

Tony..

You hear that people, I am the work of God. Kneel before me.

8) fghtytyytyt, 38 years old from Amador City, CA

Hello pretty looks

My name is micheal scott, I saw your profile and It is very nice and I will like to get to know you.. I am very new to this online dating thing , I just sign in here some days ago, I am looking here to find my soul mate. I am very outgoing Honest , hardworking , who love's to go out and have a good time. I am looking forward to meet a matured, devoted,honest , caring , faithful , loving and very loyal and understanding woman . I was always told that beauty is in the eyes of the Beholder. Today, I can truely say if I was asked to define beauty i'd say it's you. I'm not refering to your physical beauty NO. the minute

I saw your profile and went through it, It is as if God opened my soul, my spirit , my heart , my every essence of being, Just so i can truely comprehend the glory of your inner beauty. I know what I want when I see what I want. and I definitely know why I need a woman in my life,cos right now i am ready to settle down I pray that my words will touch the depts of your heart. Cos its the only way you will truely know and believe that we maybe Soulmates. If you really believe in LOVE, If you want to have a future with a man who naturally knows your heart, then take my heart and let embark on a journey of bliss pleasure, accompanionship, friendship , growth, love, and beautiful family. . I am looking forward to your reply so that we can get to know each other right away and even better, If you allow me add you to my yahoo messenger or better still you add me, so that we can get to know each other better..
xxxx@yahoo.com
hope to talk with you over there
hugs and kisses.xoxoxoxoxoxoxoxoxoxo

micheal

Michael Scott?? The Michael Scott from Dunder Mifflin in Scranton, PA?

9) eric_morries40, 38 years old from Santa Rosa Beach, FL

Hi Angel,
First, I wonna confess that U're really an angel that no man can easily ignore. well Angel, i saw ur profile, and really appreciate and move by what I saw. My daddy

once told me that love is the appetite of generation by the mediation of beauty,but I never belived that not until I saw ur profile this evening. Wish U can just give me some chance to get acquinted with U, and prove to U what love really mean.
U know the fountain mingles with the river,the river with the ocean; the wings of heaven forever mix with a sweet emotion;All things in live by a law divine forever mingles with one another;Nothing in live is single;So why not U and I? Anyway, bye for now, have a nice and lovely time,and take good care of urself. Can reach, or contact me via my mail-xxxx@yahoo. com. hope to hear from you soon
SEE YEAH!

Dear Eric, does your daddy know you got into his computer?

Call the Authorities
Obsession, You Are My Obsession

We're just down right scared.

1) **wilpet01, 43 years old from Upi, GU**
   Hello Dear,
   I want to be the first person to greet you on this special day. You may wonder what day I am talking about, but believe me, any day this letter gets to you will truly be a special one for me and you are the reason why. When I went through your profile and saw your picture, I came up with this little idea when my perfect under the stars to paint a picture of you so I rummaged through the closets until I found all the old plain and blinking candle light I could find and I tacked them to the ceiling in my room. I then hauled most of my bedroom furniture to the attic. I drug in all of my plants and a couple of fake potted trees from the patio to make a picture of us together. I took the sheet off my bed. I was like this is my dream come true and would love to cook a candle light dinner for you with champagne on the side. How is life over there? Hope

all is cool. If so doxology. If given the opportunity I would put you first in my life and this comes straight from my heart and I believe you are God sent and I would love to know more about you and wish you could swim with me in this ocean called life and i think I am sure with you there will be no trouble finding love. I will like to know more about you if you don't mind here is my email addy xxxx@yahoo.com you can mail me anytime. I hope to chat with you someday. Looking forward to reading from you soon. Thanks and be cool.

Love
Wilson

Dear Wilson, what the hell is doxology?

2) **latebloomer518, 41 years old from North Hollywood, CA**

Hey Stace,
Is that really you? It says you are 36 but, to me, you look like a freshman in college. Old picture.....or just really good, youthful genetics in your family?

I am not blowing smoke or trying some cheap come-on. You have to have heard this many, many times before.

You are actually the FIRST person I've met on an online dating service that I think is looking for an older man to meet.....so, going the untraditional route.....you are lying UP about your age (as opposed to all the other women who lie DOWN about their age).

Tell me if you think I'm wrong about this.

Trust me.....I don't dislike 23 year old women....I am just somewhat skeptical. What if you were 23? Or 19? Or, God forbid, 17?

Just want to know the big picture.

Apart from that, how are you, what kinds of music and art do you like?

If I haven't frightened you with the third degree about you age, please get back to me.

Most sincerely,

Michael

Michael, FIRST of all, only my friends call me Stace. SECOND, you might want to try not calling a woman a LIAR to see if that gets you anywhere.

3) **heartcare, 41 years old from Seattle, WA**
My Name is Mark XXXX i was just glancing through and i came across your attractive profile, I have been depart for 6yrs now.. wow i must confess you are pretty, has anyone ever told you how ravishing you look? Well if not I guess am the first to do so cos I cant just stop looking at your pics and thinking that YOU WERE MINE...

Well am New here and Looking for a love and caring Lady who is ready for a serious relationship, well I just started this online dating thing which I thought I should try out and see if I would meet the right person for me, well am willing to relocate if right lady who is interested in serious Relationship comes my way. I THINK I HAVE if you are me....well if u don't mind we can chat on yahoo to get to know each other my im is william4realcare.....hope to read from u on there.... remain beautiful as always.....Mark.

Hello, 911? I think I'm being stalked.

4) **maiden2, 50 years old from Los Angeles, CA**
Like your picture and I thoght that It said that you were 50 and I was saying dame she's hot for fifiy and I gotta meet and see her and than I looked again and it said that you were 36 and you still look hot moma so email me back if color is not a issue meaning that I'm a good looking black man who thinks that you are hot moma c'mon

Dear maiden2, color isn't an issue but stupidity is.

5) **romanticideas1, 39 years old from Los Angeles, CA**
Hi thanks for the message, i am new on black planet, i am on this site looking for long term relationship with a serious woman that she kind faithful open minded loyal caring loving trustworthy with a great sence of humor a woman who will love me for who i am, i will like to chat to u lot more better so will can know everything about each other, u can IM me on

my yahoo instant messenger and here is my id, xxxx@yahoo.com what is yours as well so will can add each other and talk on yahoo messenger Now

Dear romanticideas1, sooooo, how are things on the black planet?

6) **inhumano, 36 years old from Los Angeles, CA**
Hi my name is CArlos, maybe maybe we could be friends please, email me xxxx@yahoo.com, We could leave to go anywhere Or perhaps we could have an appointment to go to the cinema...
I am a Latino Guy please email me

TK Carlos

Dear Carlos, thanks, but my cinema appointments are all booked.

7) **larry_tyler, 42 years old from Los Angeles, CA**
Hi angel,
How are you doing am larry tyler, when i was going through my system i now came accross a raving queen like you on my internet i belive i admire your beauty I'm writing to let you know how I feel about you. I don't know how to tell you , so I am going to put my feelings in words, on this page. Since the day I met you, I haven't been the same. My feelings I just can't seem to tame. I am starting to care for you in a different way. I think of you every day! I love everything about you! Your smile, your eyes, your hair, your body, etc... I am pretty sure you got the point. I can't get you off

my mind, damn, Baby Boy, you got me feeling stupid, because I know you may not feel the same, but my feelings just keep growing each and every day. Well, and I am falling in love with you - yes, this is true! But I understand if you don't feel the same. I know this sounds lame, but I have to let you know how I really feel. sometime I wake up every morning with thoughts of you in my head. Sometimes I wonder if I dreamed you up, but then I roll over and see your smiling face and I know that you're real. It's not a dream anymore. I know I can make you mad, but you still love me with everything you have. I was scared to love you at first, fearing that you would hurt me, but I dove right in and it's the best choice I've ever made. Now, the only fear I have is rolling over one morning and finding that you were really just a dream. If this is a dream world, then don't wake me up 'cause you're the only one for me. I love you with everything I have. please i will you to send me a mail or add me in your messager so that we can talk and know each other more better. please this is my private mail xxx@yahoo.com .Am expecting to read from you soon. Have a nice day babe hoping to hear from you soon.

Dear Larry, damn Baby Boy – come on, is this really Flava Flav?

8) onegoodman, 52 years old from Boca Raton, FL

Sometimes in life, bad things happen to good people. I'd have to say I'm one of them. Having put all of my trust in the love of my life, I lost everything I ever achieved--house, business, savings, the list goes on.

Undeterred I continue forward, with no baggage or haunting memories to debilitate me. I am stronger for the experience, and much wiser. Although I have not much materially or financially to offer, I have an abundance of personality, wit, humor, sensitivity and perhaps most importantly honesty. I am as faithful as a lab--and as lovable as one. I've been told I'm pretty darn cute too. I would like to meet my soul mate. A woman not so concerned with the material aspects of my offerings as she is with the spiritual and emotional makeup of who I am. For this reason I hope to find a woman who is financially so secure, that my income, assets and finances are of no concern. In return she will be constantly entertained by my unique persona, unmatched comical nature and...this is the best part... unwavering love and emotional support. One thing's for sure...You will not be disappointed.

Dear onegoodman, you are right - bad things happen to good people. I was recently laid off from my job, moved to Florida from L.A., staying with my family and collecting unemployment. Still interested?

9) buddyrich49, 49 years old from Fort Lauderdale, FL

I hope you read my post. I'm very real and not a player to hurt you. I'm recently been financially hurt bad by a divorce.I looking hard for work and trying to put my life back together. I miss taking emotionally care of a special Lady. You are very beautiful and would not be dissapointed with the way I would treat you(in every way). Loyaty and Honor is what I live with everyday.

Einstein said that "Imagination is more important than Knowledge" Either Einstein or Newton said that"To rate a man not by his worth value but by the values of the man.
God Bless you,

Richard

Dear Richard, Einstein knew how to spell. And God Bless you as well.

10) bostonbob11n, 48 years old from West Palm Beach, FL

(this was via text after exchanging information)

Bb: hi so I know ur cute but not your name
Robin: sorry I thought I signed my name on my email. it's robin
Bb: what a coincidence. Im batman. I bet we make a good team
Robin: lol
Bb: so what brings you to okcupid?
Robin: I'm not on okcupid. I'm on plenty of fish
Bb: I meant pof. so ur cute an funny
Robin: I'm a laugh a minute
Bb: uh oh
Robin: what brought you to pof
Bb: cute funny girls have any luck so far
Robin: I haven't been on that long. met some interesting people though.
Bb: guys are idiots but I'm not. ask me anything.
Robin: can we talk later.

Bb: sure pick a topic
Robin: how bout a lite get to know you phone call
Bb: so we are going to save the convo about my meth lab and porn addiction for another time?
Robin: yep. and we will never bring up my five ex-husbands who all died under mysterious circumstances
Bb: deal.are u 420 friendly?
Robin: ummmmm..what?
Bb: do you like pot?
Robin: no
Bb: okay no biggie

Dude, it is a biggie. You are 48-years-old and feel the need to throw it out there that pot is a HUGE part of your life. I had to go to my urban dictionary to find out what the hell 420 meant. Well, schizzel my mcnizzle – it's legalize pot day. Word!

Disclaimer
We're Not Experts or Endorsers

Well, folks, there it is – the good, bad and ugly of online dating. We hope you enjoyed our collection and want to take this opportunity to remind everyone that we aren't making any claims, good or bad, with this book. We don't have doctorates in psychology or sociology and don't consider ourselves "relationship experts." We're just two women who used online dating sites and discussed it with others. While we're half expecting singlesnet to ask Stacey and Jason to film a commercial for them, we are not endorsed by any of the sites mentioned in this book. Although unemployment is still an issue, so don't be shy, singlesnet.